NEVER TOO LATE
TO LOVE

David Torkington has sold over
400,000 books and been translated
into 13 languages.

BOOKS BY DAVID TORKINGTON

The Primacy of Loving – The Spirituality
of the Heart

Wisdom from The Christian Mystics –
How to Pray the Christian Way

Wisdom from the Western Isles –
The Making of a Mystic

Wisdom from Franciscan Italy –
The Primacy of Love

How to Pray – A Practical Guide
to the Spiritual Life

Prayer Made Simple – CTS booklet

Inner Life – A Fellow Traveller's Guide
to Prayer

A New Beginning – A Sideways Look at
the Spiritual Life

Dear Susanna – It's Time for a Christian
Renaissance

His website is https://www.davidtorkington.com

NEVER TOO LATE TO LOVE

Our Lady's Sublime Teaching on Prayer

DAVID TORKINGTON

MERCIER PRESS

Mercier Press, 82c Ballyhooly Road, St. Luke's, Cork, Ireland

Published by Mercier Press, 2025
Copyright © David Torkington, 2023

The moral rights of David Torkington to be identified as the author of this work have been asserted in accordance with the Copyright and Related Rights Act, 2000.

Ebook ISBN: 9781917453745
Original Edition ISBN: 9781917453486
Hardcover ISBN: 9781806900336
Large Print ISBN: 9781806900381
Cover design by The Sisters at the Benedictines of Mary, Queen of Apostles

To Our Lady of Mount Carmel

Praise For Never Too Late To Love: Our Lady's Sublime Teaching on Prayer

This book on Prayer, written by David Torkington, is a precious help for all who seriously desire to pray in a godly manner and to live a life of grace-filled supernatural union with God. This book does not whitewash the evidence of the real historical situation in which Catholics are currently living, and this is its merit and honest advantage. The following assertions of the author represent, in my opinion, the gist of his work: "Before Catholic tradition used the wisdom of God to change the world, but now the wisdom of the world is being used to change Catholic tradition. In this new world order there is only egality and fraternity for those who have rejected all laws, all standards, all morals and manners that once made human society possible. The rest are consigned to oblivion or modern versions of the guillotine. Unless in this, the final moments of 'injury time' the love that endlessly flows from the Sacred Heart of the Queen of heaven is received, welcomed, and assimilated, then disaster is awaiting." The core message of this book affirms that the true renewal, the true gift of Pentecost consists in the following: being God-centred, prayer-centred according to the model of the Immaculate Heart of Mary and possessing the richness of an interior life through prayer, sacrifice and love. This alone will make all pastoral activities bear lasting fruit and provide us here on earth through Our Lady's sublime teaching on prayer a foretaste of the eternal beatitude in God. I believe that this book will bring great spiritual good for the readers, for which we are grateful to David Torkington.

+ Athanasius Schneider, Auxiliary Bishop of the Archdiocese of Saint Mary in Astana

David Torkington is a man who understands Catholic mystical tradition. If you will allow him, he will lead you into the depths of prayer and into the heart of God.

+ Dan Burke - Founder of the Avila Institute for Spiritual Formation and the community of Apostoli Viae

David Torkington's treatise is a great help for Catholics and non-Catholics alike, who are seeking deeper union with God through His own Blessed Mother's intercession and lessons on prayer. There is such richness in these pages, that I hope many will read and partake of the feast offered herein; words that draw us closer to the Word made Flesh Who still dwells amongst us. There is no doubt that great peace of soul will result among hearts open to receiving this inspired wisdom.

+ Mother Abbess Cecilia, Benedictines of Mary, Queen of Apostles

13

Contents

FOREWORD

I KNOW HOW HARD IT IS learning to pray, even for those (like me) who grew up reading the Scriptures. You know the stories of the Gospel, you know the letters of the Apostles and the scenes of heavenly prayer in Revelation, but somehow knowing the stories and lessons does not automatically translate into practice, even when you recite the Lord's Prayer. Shouldn't there be angels singing, visions of the Throne, ecstasies, and transfigurations as you breathe the words, 'Thy will be done, on earth as it is in heaven?'

'Clearly,' you worry, 'I'm doing it wrong.'

Growing up Presbyterian, I assumed others must know better how to access such ecstasies of prayer, particularly those familiar with Our Lady. I am not sure why I thought to assume this, except when I travelled to

Europe for the first time in high school and found myself at Chartres wondering at the life of faith that inspired its architects and artists. How, I wondered, might I gain access to the love of Our Lady shining through the jewel-like glass of her windows? Even more to the point, why had medieval Christians focused so much on Mary when surely, as Christians, they worshipped not her, but her Son?

When I was received into the Catholic Church six years ago, I was startled to learn that much of the mystery I sensed at Chartres has been lost not just to Presbyterians, but even to modern Catholics. David Torkington's interview with Patrick Coffin for Hope Is Fuel and the present book have helped me to understand why: since the late seventeenth century, the fear of Quietism has driven out of the Church many of the practices on which the medieval devotion to Our Lady depended, ironically including the very prayers through which medieval Christians expressed their love of the Blessed Virgin as the Ark and Temple of the presence of Christ.

'O Lady,' St. Anselm of Canterbury (d. 1109) memorably prayed, 'you showed to the world its Lord and its God whom it had not known. You showed to the sight of all the world its Creator whom it had not seen.' Mary is the one who nudges us to pray; she is, as I have experienced in my own scholarship and conversion, the one who is constantly there, pressing us gently as she did her Son: 'They have no wine.' 'You need to pray.' In the Middle Ages, monks and nuns who felt the nudge developed practices modelled on the Divine Office by which to honour her, beginning in the late tenth century with cycles of psalms (the so-called Little Office of the Virgin) and over the course of the following centuries, adding simplified versions of its chants and prayers to their daily devotions. Modern Catholics will be familiar with one of these, the Rosary, itself focused on the antiphon with which the Little Office of the Virgin opens: 'Hail, Mary, full of grace, the Lord is with thee.'

By the later Middle Ages, every Christian who knew how to read would have known these prayers because—thanks to Our Lady's nudges—they would have learned how to read using books of Hours containing the psalms of her Office. These are the same Hours by which Christians prayed in antiquity, remembering the events of the Passion over the course of each day, the hours of the day sanctified by meditation on Our Lord's suffering. And yet, at no point were these devotions meant to be at all burdensome, as the miracles granted to Mary's devotees constantly emphasized. Simply saying the Ave Maria regularly brings great delight to Our Lady, reminding her (as one famous miracle story told it) of the joy she had in the moment when the angel Gabriel first greeted her and she conceived Our Lord in her womb.

It is a great joy to hear and read David Torkington's encouragement for modern Catholics to take up these prayers. Simple as they are, they contain the whole of prayer, much as Mary contained the Creator of the world in her womb. I think now, after studying these prayers in my scholarship and taking them up in my own practice, I have at least a glimmer of an inkling of what inspired the builders of Chartres, but just as the rose windows shine always new with the light streaming through them, so Mary, our rose window, shines ever Virgin with the glory of her Son—and rejoices to hear us say, 'Ave'.

As it turns out, learning to pray is much easier than I thought. All it takes is a nudge from our Mother.

Let us pray!

Rachel Fulton Brown

INTRODUCTION

The time for fence-sitting is over. Very
many hundreds of thousands, if not millions,
of our early Christian forebears, suffered
imprisonment, torture, and frightening and
horrendous deaths for the faith that we
take all too easily for granted. All too many
are prepared to stand by as our faith is
being stripped away from us by Catholics
who, in the early Church, would have long
since been excommunicated for flouting
the teaching of Christ in such serious ways.
They would simply not be in positions of
the highest authority remaking the Church,
not in the image and likeness of God and
his Kingdom of Love, but in their own image
and likeness. They dress up their heretical
theology in the language of traditional
Catholic teaching and gaslight the naïve
and the unwary into accepting it as the new
orthodoxy.

Today's modernism, which is man's own creation, had its roots in the birth of the modern world, usually seen as the Renaissance. Let us see then how the original God-given theology that Christ gave us has been subtly replaced by the anthropocentric theology that man has given to himself.

An important meeting took place in Florence in 1350 that posterity has seen as symbolising the beginning of the Renaissance, the birth of the modern world, or Humanism. It was a meeting of two great Latin scholars, Petrarch and Boccaccio. Their love of what was in danger of becoming a dead language reintroduced not just its splendour but the splendours of the ancient classical world that it re-presented to its readers. It sparked off an interest in all things classical that were the glory of the Greco-Roman culture that was lost to sight in the 'Dark Ages.'

Although this new trend could be seen portrayed in the architecture and the art that thrived in the following two centuries, it could also be experienced in the new cultural ideas and ideals which heralded a new era in which man and his position in the world began to take centre stage. The fact that this new world view began in the immediate aftermath of the Great Plague (1348-9) that took the lives of almost half of Europe was not insignificant. A Christian world that had, to date, an unerring belief in God and in his loving mercy began to despair, think again, and look elsewhere for ways on which to base their religious lives. They began to look more to themselves and to their own resources for personal 'salvation' and to Humanism of one sort or another that was already in its infancy.

Thanks to Petrarch and Boccaccio and their many followers, they were able to discover the old philosophical 'religions' like Stoicism, Neoplatonism, Manichaeism, and inevitably semi-Pelagianism, amongst others. They all had one thing in common: they depended not on God's power but on their own power for the 'spiritual' advancement they sought. Henceforth, in Christianity, two distinct emphases travelled forward into the future side by side: the old emphasis that was centred not on man but on God and his power and glory, and the new emphasis that was centred on man and his power and glory. The Credo of the old order was 'I believe in God'. The Credo of the new order was 'I believe in Man'. In subsequent centuries, the theocentric religion that had been introduced by Jesus Christ at the dawn of Christianity gradually began to be infiltrated by the new emphasis on man and his new anthropocentric religious ideas.

I want to show by reductio ad absurdum or by reducing this new anthropocentric emphasis in our beloved Catholic Church to its absurdity how we have now arrived at the moral malaise in which the contemporary Church finds herself.

Let me begin with St Thomas Aquinas and with his simple but profound statement with which he summed up not just the essence of the new Dominican order to which he belonged but the Catholic Faith that Jesus Christ bequeathed to his followers. His timeless words were these: 'Our calling is to Contemplate and to share the fruits of Contemplation with others.' Although the first Christians did not use the language later associated with mystical theology, they all knew that they were called not just to be taken up into the Mystical Body of Christ but there to be prepared and purified through prayer to participate in Christ's own mystical contemplation of his Father. In doing this, they would receive the fruits of that contemplation.

Contemplating the God of Love, in, with, and through Christ, is the only way to receive the fullness of his love in return. This is the love that contains within it all the infused virtues and the gifts and fruits of the Holy Spirit, beginning with the wisdom that Christ promised they would receive after his glorification (John 14:25-27). This wisdom was not reserved for the Catholic intelligentsia but for all, even the humblest followers of Christ, through what came to be called the sensus fidelium.

After the Renaissance, however, the new anthropocentric trend that seeped into the new activity-centred congregations that arose before and after the Council of Trent played down, if not positively rejected, the profound contemplative spirituality that Jesus Christ first practised and then introduced into the early Church.

This God-given spirituality that was the heart and soul of the ancient monastic orders and later mendicant orders like the Dominicans, the Franciscans, the Carmelites, and the

Augustinians was not embodied in the new activity-centred congregations. For them, the mystical contemplation into which Christ had called his first followers was literally a nonstarter. Following the lead of St Ignatius in his Exercises that were deeply infected by the new anthropocentric humanistic spirituality, meditation on the life of Christ came to be called contemplation. Whereas, in the past, meditation was only seen as the way, the means, that leads to true mystical contemplation.

It also therefore came to be seen as an end in itself, as the height of a believer's personal prayer life, after which they would prematurely set out 'to set the world on fire' before the only purification that could alone spiritually change them. The misnomer, 'contemplation in action', is all but a contradiction in terms, an oxymoron. It is a cosy, comfortable little phrase that has for centuries misled millions into believing that they can transform others with the love of God that has yet to transform themselves. The Latin epigram, Nemo enim dat quod non habet, says it all. In other words, you cannot give to others what you have not received yourself. That is why Jesuits who are inspired by their traditional Humanistic 'spirituality' have been compared, 'in their day' to the contemporary Charismatic movement, at least when it fails to move on, like its counterpart in the early Church, into contemplative prayer. It was this sublime prayer that was seen perfectly embodied in their mentor and mother, Mary Immaculate, on the first Pentecost day and thereafter on every other day. The prolonged mystical contemplation in which a believer would be purified, to be united with Christ's contemplation of his Father, that was the heart and soul of the older orders, plays no official part in Ignatian spirituality or that of those who are influenced by them. When the then General of the Jesuit congregation, Mercurian, heard that one of his Jesuits was supporting St Teresa of Avila in her contemplative prayer, he was told to return her immediately to following the 'Ignatian Exercises'. It was like telling a PhD student to return to their elementary school, a school incidentally riddled with Humanism. Militant evangelical Jesuits have been doing this ever since.

According to Monsignor Ronald Knox and other experts, the profound mystical theology that Christ himself introduced into the early Church reached a high point in the older orders in the seventeenth century (See Enthusiasm Chapter XI page 232). Then, it suddenly declined. The condemnation of Molinos and his counterfeit 'Mysticism', Quietism in 1687 put all forms of mystical contemplation, including the works of St Teresa of Avila and St John of the Cross, under suspicion (See A Short History of the Catholic Church by Monsignor Philip Hughes page 184).

The anti-mystical witch hunts that followed, together with the spirit of the New Age of Enlightenment that seeped into the Church, rejected mystical prayer where loving is leant through selfless giving and took the heart and soul out of authentic Catholic Spirituality. In the last four hundred years or so, authentic Catholic mystical prayer, where selfless loving is learnt under the tutelage of the Holy Spirit, has been seriously undermined. It has been undermined despite the attempts of the great Dominican spiritual theologian Garrigou-Lagrange to restore it. It has been almost totally infiltrated by an anthropocentric spirituality that can be seen most clearly in Jesuit spirituality.

I am only explicitly citing the Jesuits because, since the Council of Trent, they have increasingly become the most numerous and the most dominant and the most influential religious congregation. They are the most evangelical in promoting an anti-evangelical spirituality which is too closely allied to semi-Pelagianism for comfort. This means that their official spirituality is totally bereft of the perennial Catholic teaching on mystical theology that has been the lifeblood of the Church from the beginning, with Mary the first Christian mystic on the first Pentecost day. However, they are by no means exclusively to blame. Particularly after the condemnation of Quietism, the older orders like the Dominicans and the Franciscans have increasingly forgotten their contemplative origins, and so without the fruits of contemplation, they gradually became only nominal practitioners of the virtues to which they aspire. In early Dominican spirituality, for instance, inspired by St Dominic and instructed by St Thomas Aquinas, they knew that the reception of the infused virtues did not precede contemplation but primarily proceeded from the practice of contemplation.

Although, therefore, today, they still insist
on the importance of attaining the virtues,
without the practice of the contemplation
that has all but vanished from Catholic
Spirituality, they can only try to attain them
like the Jesuits, by their own endeavour.
In short, like stoics and not like Christians
inspired by their mother, Mary. The fact
of the matter is that because the true
contemplation in which the infused virtues
are received has long since disappeared, so
also has the reception of their God-given
supernatural fruits. Hence, the spiritual
malaise that prevails today. Sadly, this
profound form of prayer, which St Thomas
Aquinas used to distinguish his fellow
Dominicans, only remains in theory but not
in practice. That is why, with the 'sensus
fidelium' as their guide, the young are no
longer inspired to join in any numbers those
orders once committed to a contemplative
spirituality and many who do eventually
leave. Since I went to try my vocation in the

Franciscan order, for instance, before the Second Vatican Council, a province of over three hundred has diminished to hardly more than ten active friars.

Although the Second Vatican Council did restore the ancient liturgical expression of early Christian spirituality, it did nothing either to secure and safeguard its solemnity, its essential sacrificial character or to restore the God-given contemplative spirituality of which it was the expression. This failure left religious orders and congregations in a state of disarray, for they all felt they had lost their way and so countless hundreds of priests and religious left during the nineteen sixties and seventies. With the avowed objective of helping them recover their charisms, Jesuit missionaries, or their delegates, tried to imbue them with their own modern anthropocentric form of Humanism. Following their age-old tradition of harnessing not God's Wisdom but the wisdom of the world, they introduced to the sheep without shepherds the latest secular wisdom for their spiritual advancement. Myriad methods of pop socio-psychological methods and techniques would do for them what the Holy Spirit did before. Prayer, in general, and mystical theology, in particular, was out. Self-improvement courses of every shape and form, no matter how bizarre, were in. The catastrophic consequences for religious life are well known, but they have never been fully quantified. In the name of modernity, the Jesuits have, since their general chapter of 1963, recognised that their soft Humanism had failed, and they prepared to introduce hard Humanism, which turned the hierarchical structure of their order upside down and further humanised their Apostolic orientation.

This is shown quite clearly by Fr Malachi Martin, a one-time Jesuit himself, in his book, The Jesuits. He shows how they then imported a new religious agenda culled from liberation theology and primitive Marxism. However, they subtly camouflaged their duplicity by using traditional Catholic terminology and misinterpretations of the scriptures to deceive the unwary. Revelation, which once had its source in God in heaven, is now to be sought from the people on earth or, to use a now commonly accepted Catholic phrase, 'the people of God' in order to try and keep on board traditional believers. 'The people', they argue, are far better positioned to see how revelation has changed to accommodate the signs of modern times. As the very few who have been consulted are a little slow to read these signs correctly, specially chosen 'evangelical' collators' have been on hand to help them to come to the conclusions to which they, together with their mentors, have already come! The conclusions of the Synods to come, then, have already been decided before the highly expensive charade of consultation began! You can fool some of the people for some of the time, but let's hope they cannot be fooled for all of the time.

The spiritual chaos that depleted religious life and the priesthood in the latter part of the twentieth century left a gap where chaos and anarchy reigned supreme, most particularly amongst those to whom the faithful have traditionally looked for leadership. It has been the perfect opportunity for what is known as the Marx/Lenin principle to be enacted. In short, a small group of revolutionaries knowing exactly what they want can take over the reins of power when anarchy reigns supreme. Such a group of high-ranking religious and priests who recently emerged from the chaos have now, in the third decade of the twenty-first century, taken power, bent on consolidating their position and introducing into the Catholic Church the latest wisdom of the world in the

form of a radical LGBTQ agenda, together with the new secular religion of globalism, otherwise known as the New World Order. In the early Church, this agenda would have excommunicated all involved and so anathematised all their pronouncements, releasing the faithful from observing the subsequent decrees.

As they have long since rejected the true infused virtue of Wisdom that only comes through receiving the fruits of mystical contemplation, as St Thomas Aquinas insists, they have introduced a man-made and deeply flawed method of seeking the truth called 'discernment'. The process can be manipulated like a Ouija board to obtain the results that have been decided upon before the process begins. A smokescreen of religious rites and rituals deceives the naïve and the unwary into believing that the results that have been predetermined are of God and, therefore, all but infallible.

In brief, the same method that destroyed so many religious communities in the last century is now being used to destroy the Church itself in the twenty-first century. This is the absurdity into which the now totally dominant anthropocentric spirituality has led us. Before, Catholic tradition used the wisdom of God to change the world, but now, the wisdom of the world is being used to change Catholic tradition.

How sad and ironical that a former Master General of the Dominican order has been asked to preside over a retreat to prepare the participants for the Synod in October 2023. Here, an LGBTQ agenda has been adopted, using the long-since discredited and exploitable method of discernment that is alien to the spirit and practice of the order over which the retreat master once presided. For the great Dominican, Thomas Aquinas, and for the whole authentic Catholic spiritual tradition, true wisdom is only given to those who, after sufficient purification in prayer, have been drawn into Christ's own contemplation of the Father. It is only then that the Holy Spirit is able to fill believers with the infused virtues, enabling Him to suffuse his wisdom into those who seek it for the good of the Church, which is helpless without it. I will say no more about these matters here as I have dealt with them at length in my book, The Primacy of Loving.

There is, however, hope for what I am sad to say may be the few, 'the happy few', the remnant who want to fuel their hope with true Catholic Wisdom and spiritual orthodoxy. I was overawed by Fr Malachy Martin's brilliant analysis in his book, The Jesuits. He details how his beloved Jesuit congregation committed spiritual suicide when their general Chapter of 1973 proclaimed their plans for their hardline humanistic future. However, I found it impossible to agree with him about the way forward to genuine Catholic renewal. He believed that both the Vatican Council and its aftermath could be redeemed and the Church successfully renewed if only the then thirty-thousand-plus army of Jesuits could have been unleashed to transform the Church and the world simultaneously with their old-style Ignatian spiritual tradition. If what I have already said does not make this abundantly clear as a complete non-starter, then my book, The Primacy of Loving, will make this plain in no uncertain terms.

It seems to me that there are two clear ways forward. The first is to go back over all the intervening successes and failures of the last two thousand years or more to the simple but profound God-given theology and spirituality that Jesus Christ Our Lord introduced into the early Church. This was, and still is, a spirituality that is most perfectly embodied in Our Lady. Although it

is this theocentric theology and spirituality
that has inspired all my books, it is most
particularly detailed in my next book, Family
Spirituality – Christ's Gift to his Church,
published by Essentialist Press. It details
the perennial Catholic spirituality from the
beginning. The second way is to immediately
begin to practise this spirituality as it has
been perfectly summarised for us by Our
Lady in her genuine appearances over the
last hundred years or so. In the book that
you are about to read, I will explain how this
spirituality is perfectly summed up in the
four words: Repentance, Prayer, Sacrifice,
and the Mass, with the Rosary standing out
as the primary means of prayer. Everyone
can follow Our Lady's simple but sublime
summary of early Christian Spirituality,
beginning immediately and now.

It means going back to the future, back to
the simple, clear, and coherent God-centred
Spirituality that Jesus Christ introduced into

the early Church, a spirituality that oozed out of the writings of the early Fathers of the Church. It is this spiritual orthodoxy that inspired me and all that I have written over the last fifty years. It is my hope and prayer that it will inspire all Catholics who, unbeknown to the vast majority, are about to be seduced by modernism gone mad using the latest Marxist strategy to take over the Church as it is trying to take over the Western world. At Fatima, Our Lady said that her Immaculate Heart will be her gift to the Church in the difficult times that are now upon us. It is this promise, above all, that has inspired me to write this book.

David Torkington

Chapter 1

Our Lady's Message

THE GREEK PHILOSOPHER PLATO said that although we have emerged from being cave dwellers, built great cities to live in, and decorated them with beautiful artistic masterpieces, we still live spiritually like cave dwellers. We live in a world of shadows, blind to the most important truths that could really change our lives. We have lived in this world of shadows for so long, he said, that when someone comes to tell us the truth, we do not want to know, do not want to listen, and if they keep pestering us, we become angry. And if they persist and keep trying to tell us the truth that we do not want to hear, we put them to death, as they put Socrates, his mentor, to death.

His fellow countrymen had, for years, believed in over two thousand different gods, but Socrates said there could only be one, so, in the end, they called him an atheist and put him to death for perverting the young. Four hundred years later, Jesus Christ came to tell everyone the truth and, like Socrates before him, was condemned to death because they did not want to hear it. Socrates wanted all who listened to him to live the good, virtuous lives that would make them happy, as did Jesus. But Jesus was able to help them to live good, virtuous lives by giving those who listened to him the power to do it.

He was able to do this because he was not just a man but the Son of God, a God of love. It was this love that would make what was impossible to the followers of Socrates possible. Without love, even the best of men and women would never succeed in living good, virtuous lives for long. That is why, when their descendants saw the followers of Jesus filled with love and living the good, virtuous lives that they were unable to maintain, they asked to join their ranks.

Gradually, Christians began to forget what Jesus taught, and what was once a powerful, vibrant faith began to decline. Although in subsequent centuries, there were many new and successful beginnings, decline usually set in again. By the time the twentieth century arrived, things were so bad that short of some sort of heavenly intervention, it seemed nothing could be done to save not just unbelievers but believers, too, from perdition. That intervention came many times over in the person of Our Lady, the Mother of God. She has appeared many times to young children to tell them once more the truth that the adult world to which they belonged had forgotten. It was exactly the same message that Jesus gave, and that had been lived out in the early Church but explained so simply that the children and those to whom they related the message could understand it too.

The four words that sum up the message that Our Lady delivered to the children at her appearances can be expressed as a single word: love. The first, to 'Repent' means to turn back to the love of God and then keep turning to receive what can alone change our lives permanently for the better. The genuine happiness and joy it brings will enable us to share what we have received with others. For the first Jews, there was no such thing as someone who has repented, but only for someone who is repenting and who continues to repent or who turns to God and who keeps turning to God to receive his love in return. It is a lifelong action of loving that continues every day for the rest of our lives, in and out of formal prayer, through all and everything we say and do and all whom we try to love and serve.

That is why the second word that Our Lady uses to sum up a life of loving God is the word 'Sacrifice'. In order to do this, you have to give up a hundred and one other things that you would prefer to do for your own personal pleasure and satisfaction. So, a truly Catholic life is a life full of sacrifices, not done for their own sake or to show how you can make yourself perfect, like the stoics, but to show how, like Mary herself, everything that is said or done is done for the love of God.

The third word she uses to describe that loving is 'Prayer'. Why? It is because prayer is the place and the time set aside to practise repentance, to practise sacrificing in concentrated periods of time set aside for that purpose. It is rather like a spiritual gymnasium. People use a secular gymnasium to prepare their physical bodies to enable them to act with ever greater ease and facility through the rest of the day. However, it is in endlessly trying to turn back to God in the spiritual gymnasium which is prayer, by repeatedly turning away from the distractions and temptations that are always there, that our sacrificial loving is not only practised but fused and surcharged with the fruits of Christ's own sacrificial loving. It is here, then, that a person is made capable of doing all things possible for God, even the impossible.

The final word that sums up her message for the modern world is the word, 'Eucharist' or the Mass. It is here that what has been primarily done in private is done in public with all other Catholics present, offering all the sacrifices that have been made in practising repentance inside and outside of prayer to God. We do not do it alone because Jesus Christ himself is present during every Mass in a very special way. He is present as our ever-loving and glorified Saviour who is doing two things simultaneously. He is loving God, and he is loving us. His love for us is like a powerful mystical force that draws up all who are open to receive him into himself. Then, in him and with him, everyone is united together in his Mystical Body, to be one with each other in offering all the sacrifices made since we last came to Mass to our common Father.

But that is not all. Christ is always present to anyone who is open to him through repentance, helping us to live the same sort of sacrificial life that he led. But at Mass, he becomes present in the sacred bread and wine so that we can both physically and spiritually receive him into our hearts and minds and bodies. He does not do this as a reward for being good, but to help us to be good as he was good by continually giving us the help and strength to keep loving God every moment of our daily lives as he did.

'I praise You, Father, Lord of heaven and earth, that You have hidden these things, these spiritual truths from the wise and intelligent and revealed them to little Children' (Matthew 11:25).

CHAPTER 2

THE IMMACULATE CONCEPTION

MOST SCRIPTURE SCHOLARS would say that Our Lady was born about fifteen or sixteen years before Christ was born, but Blessed John Duns Scotus would say she was actually conceived much earlier than that. But who is John Duns Scotus, and why should we listen to him? He was born and baptised John about seven hundred years ago in Scotland in a place called Duns. That is why he came to be called John Duns Scotus or, as he is now, Blessed John Duns Scotus. In England, before the Council of Trent, it was he, not St Thomas Aquinas, who was the theologian of choice in England for those studying to become priests. However, up to the French Revolution, every Catholic University in mainland Europe had two chairs of Theology, one for professors of the

Theology of St Thomas Aquinas and the other for professors of the Theology of Blessed John Duns Scotus. I have dealt with the teaching of Scotus in more detail in my book, Wisdom from Franciscan Italy.

In this book, both these theological giants have profound insights that will help us to understand and appreciate better the teaching of Our Lady on prayer. To my understanding of Our Lady's prayer life, I would also like to add the name of my mentor, the great spiritual theologian Father Garrigou-LaGrange OP. For, without an understanding of his presentation of the deep traditional Catholic teaching on contemplation, Our Lady's own sublime contemplative life would not be fully understood, nor therefore would our own.

After becoming a Franciscan, Scotus studied at Oxford and Paris, where he made a name for himself as a great theologian and defender of Our Lady's Immaculate Conception, which, in those days, was not accepted by possibly the majority of great theologians. Because he maintained that Our Lady was conceived by God in eternity, he concluded that she must be Immaculately conceived. When God decided to create us so that other beings made of flesh and blood could share in the ecstatic bliss that he experiences, he wanted his own Son to be born into that world like everyone else, to become the King of all Creation.

In the very act of making this decision, Our Lady was first conceived because how could his only begotten Son be born on earth without a human mother? God did not, could not, have conceived a sinful human being to be the Mother of God, so she must inevitably have been conceived by God as being Immaculate from the very beginning, free of the sinfulness and the consequences of sin that other human beings fall into.

However, it was not defined as a dogma of the Church until 1854 by Pope Pius IX in the papal bull, Ineffabilis Deus. Just a few years later, Our Lady appeared to a little girl called Bernadette at Lourdes in the South of France. When she asked 'the beautiful lady' her name, she answered, 'I am the Immaculate Conception'.

The good news is that it is from Our Lady herself, the Immaculate Conception, from whom we learn the true meaning of Christian prayer. In her appearances, she did not tell the little children how she was first taught how to pray and how her prayer life deepened when she, who had first taught her own Son Jesus how to pray, learnt from him how to pray even more deeply, and even more perfectly than ever before. Instead, she summed up so perfectly the very essence of authentic Christian prayer, and she did this in only four unforgettable words that we will examine in ever greater detail. In order to do this, we are going to see how she was taught to pray. Then, how she taught her own Son, Jesus, how to pray, and how he taught her to bring her prayer to perfection, enabling us to see through her own example and practice how we should pray too, and how our prayer can be brought to perfection.

She was first taught to pray by her own mother and Father, St Anne and St Joachim. But how do we know precisely how and what they taught her? The answer is through the Talmud. After Jerusalem was destroyed by the Romans in AD 70, most of its Jewish inhabitants were scattered all over the world. Fearing that all their traditions and customs and prayers would be lost forever, they were gathered together in a book called the Talmud. From this book, we know how St Anne and St Joseph would have taught her to pray. Every day, she would have heard her Father pray what is called the Berakah at mealtimes. At minor meals, it would be comparatively short, but at major family meals and on major feast days, it would be much longer.

In this prayer, which would in early Christian times develop into what we now call the Eucharistic prayer, her Father would give thanks to God. He would give thanks not just for the food on the table but for the Promised Land given to them by God from which that food came and, most of all, for the promise that they would be God's own people. He would love them with an unconditional love and would send an anointed prophet to them, called the Messiah. He would make them into a great nation, as he had promised to Abraham. There was only one response that could be given to the indescribable benevolence of God, and that was to return his love in kind.

It was St Anne, Mary's Mother, who taught Our Lady how to do this in a prayer called the Shema. In this prayer, which would be equivalent to our Morning Offering, she would consecrate the whole day ahead of her to loving God. She would do this by praying that she would love him with her whole mind and heart, with her whole body and soul, and with her whole strength. In this way, what was the greatest of all the commandments was made into a daily prayer. The moment Our Lady awoke in the morning, she repented, continually turning to God in prayer, promising to love him throughout the forthcoming day in all she said and did. By this, I do not mean that she repented of her sins because she had not committed any. I mean that she immediately turned away from all and everything else that was likely to distract her from turning to God with her whole mind and heart. Then, she would pray the Shema to thank God for his love and all his love he had given and would give to her and her people. She did this by consecrating her mind and heart, her body and soul, and her whole strength to loving God in the forthcoming day and on every day. Then, she would be taught how to go to the synagogue three times a day to repeat this prayer with others or alone at nine o'clock in the morning, midday, and three o'clock in the afternoon and, finally, before going to bed at night. If, for whatever reason, a person could not go to the synagogue at these times, then they prayed wherever they happened to be, on pilgrimage, working, or on their sick bed or wherever.

A famous Jewish Rabbi used to say to his students that they should repent at the moment of death. When his students asked how they would know when that would be, he answered, 'You don't, so repent at every moment.' This is what a good Jew was taught to do: to keep turning to God at every moment. That is what Our Lady was taught to do by her parents, and that is what she was able to do all the time. What may be impossible to everyone else was possible to her because of her Immaculate Conception. This meant that the sin and the selfishness that prevented others never prevented her from doing what she wanted to do more than anything else.

Chapter 3

A New Type of Temple

OUR LADY WOULD HAVE KNOWN that
God was referred to as a Father in the Old
Testament and that he was called Father
thirteen times. He was the creator, the one
who made the world and everything in it and
was a rather distant Father. But, when Jesus
began to speak about God, he said that the
rather distant God, whom most people were
afraid of, was to everyone the sort of loving
Dad that Mary had come to know and love
in St Joachim and the sort of loving Dad he
himself had known in St Joseph.

Of course, Our Lady and Our Lord would
not have used the word Dad either of God
or of their own parents because they spoke
Aramaic. They would have used the word
Abba. It comes as a great surprise to most

people when you tell them that when Jesus taught the first Apostles how to say the Our Father, the word for Father was not that used by the prophets in the Old Testament, but the word he and his mother used when they referred to their own Fathers, St Joachim and St Joseph. Just as they called them Abba, Jesus taught his apostles and future followers to call God the Father Abba, or Dad, in our language. Jesus not only told people just how much their heavenly Dad loved them but that when he returned to enjoy his Dad's infinite love forever, he would not forget those left behind, and he promised they would follow him.

True to his promise and only ten days after he was reunited with his Divine Dad, he poured out the love that his Father had lavished on him onto those he had left behind. So, on the first Pentecost day, together with the apostles and over three thousand others who received this love, Our

Lady herself received it for herself. She had already received and experienced God's love through her Son whilst he was on earth, but now his love did something unimaginable for her and everyone open to receiving it. No one had been closer than Mary to Jesus while he was on earth, but with this new outpouring of his love, she came closer to him than ever before, even closer than when he was in her womb. She was taken up into what later came to be called his Mystical Body. Here, she was able to pray not just with him like before but with and in him to their common Father who never ceased to pour out his love on her Son, in whom she now lived with the closeness that even she had not experienced before. Outwardly, not a lot seemed to have changed to onlookers in her prayer life. Like the apostles and the other disciples, she still went to the synagogue three times a day to pray, at least to begin with, but although the actual content of her prayer remained very much the same, much else had changed.

The whole point of praying at nine o'clock in the morning, midday, and three o'clock in the evening was because, at those precise times, sacrifices were being made in the Temple at Jerusalem. The ideal was that those who prayed in the synagogues at these times could identify their verbal offerings with the great physical sacrifices made by priests in the Temple. But since Jesus rose from the dead, everything changed. Jesus told his followers that after his Resurrection, his own Mystical Body would be the new Temple in which there would be a new type of worship that would be far more pleasing to God than the old. We know for a fact that Our Lady and St Joseph regularly went to the Temple in Jerusalem, where they, like all orthodox Jews, offered physical sacrifices to God with the guidance of the priests. Mary and Joseph would have known, as anyone who reads the New Testament closely, that there was no evidence that Jesus ever offered physical sacrifices in the Temple. This is because he wanted to introduce a new, more interior form of sacrifice that did not involve a physical but rather a spiritual Temple (John 2:19-22).

After the Resurrection, he would be that Temple, and on the first Pentecost day, all who were open to receiving his love would be drawn up into that Spiritual Temple. Here, they would take part in a new form of worship that he first promised to the Samaritan woman. Jesus called it 'A new worship in spirit and truth' (John 4:24). It was quite distinct from the old worship that involved offering physical possessions like livestock or food to represent themselves. As Jesus made clear, what God really wants is the offering of ourselves and, more precisely, the love for him that we express in our daily prayer. This must be demonstrated and put into practice by all that we say and do each day in prayer, but also in the way we love our family and all people for whom we have been called to love as Jesus loves us. This is the true worship that God really wants when what we offer is ourselves and the person we are trying to become.

So, now, after it seemed that her beloved Son had left her, he returned to be with her more closely than ever before and more closely than with anyone else. All others who were open to receiving the love of the Risen Lord would be taken up into his Mystical Body, but none of them would be as close to him as she was. It was not just that she had been his mother on earth, but also that her Immaculate Conception meant that as she was without sin, there was nothing to hinder her from having a far more profound and complete loving relationship with him that was never fully possible on earth.

The content and pattern of her prayer did not change. Like the others, she would still pray according to the Jewish tradition at set times and places. Now, however, she was praying to God the Father, in, with and through her beloved Son, infinitely multiplying the power of her prayer and its effectiveness for others for whom she prays until the end of time. She was not only a mother to St John, according to Christ's own wishes, but also a mother to the local church over which St John presided. When she was finally assumed into heaven, she left all the restrictions of space and time behind her so that now, she was no longer just a mother to one particular church; she became a mother to the whole Church. Furthermore, her infinitely more powerful prayer could intercede for everyone in every church throughout the world and to the end of time because she is now not only the Mother of God but the Mother of the Church, too.

Chapter 4

Our Lady and Mystical Contemplation

EVERYONE HAS EXPERIENCED what it feels like to be captivated by a wonderous landscape or a gloriously calm and serene seascape that enthrals the senses. As the sun sets on the horizon, it is set aglow, emblazoning the low-lying clouds with a kaleidoscope of different shades of fiery splendour. We are still enthralled even when the light finally fades away, and darkness begins to envelop us, so we can no longer be enraptured by the beauty of God's creation. Even as we wander back into the world of hustle and bustle whence we came, the feeling of inner peace and serenity into which we were plunged remains, at least for a while.

The psychological state of awe that draws all our inner faculties together as one to search for and enjoy the beauty of God's creation is called contemplation. These enchanting experiences that we can never forget give us a brief contemplative glimpse of God through his creation and is a call to enter into the One who is the Way, the Truth, and the Life. Sadly, they are quite rare and never last long because they demand a pure and uncluttered heart which sin and selfishness have denied us.

Nevertheless, for Mary, who was immaculately conceived, that is not the case. She could, at all times, not only see the beauty of God's creation but something of the glory of God himself in a way that no other human being has been able to see and contemplate. This gift of contemplation was brought to perfection in this life when, after the sending of the Holy Spirit at Pentecost, she was not only taken up into her beloved

Son's Mystical Body but into his mystical contemplation of his Father. She was able to see and experience the love of God, not just as it is embodied in creation but as it exists in himself and in the glorious ecstatic bliss of the Three-in-One.

The word mystical simply comes from the Greek word for unseen, invisible or secret. What is called natural contemplation is used to describe the experience of gazing upon the glory of God as it can be seen embodied in his creation. The expression mystical contemplation is used to describe the experience of gazing upon the glory of God in himself—in, with and through Christ. It is because the object of this awesome contemplation is invisible and unseen that it is called mystical. Any mother wants to share with her children all that is good, beautiful and desirable that she has experienced, and the Mother of God is no exception. She wants us to be united with her Son as she is and to come to love God as he is in himself through mystical contemplation. St Thomas Aquinas insists that mystical contemplation is the penultimate pinnacle of the spiritual life because gazing upon the glory of God is the prelude to union with him.

The only way to come to know and love God as he is in himself is to begin where Our Lady herself began, by coming to love him as he was made flesh and blood in the person of her Son, Jesus Christ. That is why Our Lady became such an important person in the early Church, when, according to tradition, she settled down with her new foster Son, St John. In order that new converts could come to know Jesus as she and the other apostles and first disciples had known him, a new form of prayer arose that was later called meditation. This prayer would enable those who had not known Christ to pore over every detail of his life on earth, reflecting and ruminating on it, and so learn to know and love him.

They were taught to do this in such a way that their love for Jesus would not just impel them to become closer to him and copy him but to be united with him. Our Lady's contribution to this new form of prayer called meditation, was unique. Who else was there when she first learnt that she was to conceive the Son of God? Who else was there at his birth to tell of the moment when the infinite God became a helpless child to be laid in a manger? Who else was alive to tell of the flight into Egypt, the presentation in the Temple, and the hidden years when she was intimately involved in helping the Christ child grow in stature and in divine wisdom as he prepared for his public ministry? Who was more painfully there when he was so cruelly put to death and humiliated as a slave or as a common criminal?

That is why in the early Church, and in the present Church there is no one else who so relentlessly calls upon her children to meditate on Christ's life and, most particularly, on his Passion and death in order to come to love him. Only this love generated by loving him as he once was on earth can be transformed into a love that wants to be united with him now as he is in heaven.

This is how meditation is gradually transformed into the contemplation that enables a person to glimpse something of the glory of God, even in this life, that is the prelude to the ultimate union with God for which he created us in the first place. As the vast majority of the first Christians were Jews, it was to be expected that they would continue to pray in the synagogue three times a day until, as heretics, they were forbidden. But even then, they would meet in one another's houses to pray together three times a day. Although they used many of the same psalms, canticles, hymns, and prayers that they used before, these were gradually Christianised.

Knowing that they were now sung, recited, or prayed within the risen and Mystical Body of Jesus, their contents were often changed to reflect the new Spiritual Temple in whom they now lived and moved and had their being. Furthermore, prayer began to end with the words, 'in, with and through Our Lord Jesus Christ', or with similar words to express how they were now praying in their Risen Lord, their new Temple, and to God, their ever-loving Father.

The God, who seemed so far away before, was now near and would respond to their prayer because they were praying in, with, and through his Son, Jesus. They were taught to use the set times for daily prayer for meditation on his life and death. More precisely, we find in the writings of the early Fathers of the Church that set times for prayer, whether the faithful were together in a home or alone, should be a time for meditation too. Nine o'clock was specified as the time to meditate on Christ's infamous condemnation to death and all that this entailed, from his scourging at the Pillar to his crowning with thorns. Midday would be a reminder to meditate on all the horrors that surrounded Christ's crucifixion, and three o'clock to meditate on his actual death and the events that surrounded that terrible event.

If this is the greatest act of love for us, performed by the greatest lover the world has ever known, then it is by meditating on this action more than on any other that we can generate within us the love that can unite us within Our Risen Lord.

Chapter 5

The Sword of Suffering

OUR LADY'S TEACHING on prayer has always been the same. It is the same teaching she taught her Son as he grew up. Like everyone else born into this world, there are a hundred and one things to do to keep body and soul together each day. However, there is always time for prayer. There is time, not just for the formal prayers Our Lady was taught by her parents and the prayers that she taught her Son, but also for the deep interior personal prayer she practised and taught her Son to practise, too. When his time came to teach others, he would not only teach them to follow his example in practising the more formal daily prayers that his mother had taught him but something further.

Just as she found time daily to be alone before God and taught her Son to do the same, her Son did the same for others by both word and example. He told them to go into the 'Inner room' alone to pray to God just as he did. That would, of course, not be so easily possible when he was a travelling speaker, so he would disappear for hours at a time 'onto the mountain side' or other lonely places when he was in the countryside or when in Jerusalem into the 'garden where it was his custom to pray'. These were not just occasional sorties into solitude. They were as regular as the times his mother had prayed and taught him to pray in Nazareth.

In his Gospel, St Luke put it this way: 'His reputation continued to grow, and large crowds would gather to hear him and to have their sickness cured, but he would always go off to some place where he could be alone to pray' (Luke 5:15-16). He was taught well by his mother. Despite all her daily chores, in these precious moments when all her work was done, when all the prayers expected of her had been said, she turned to God to be lost in mystical contemplation of his sublime goodness. Compared to the one she contemplated, Mary was overcome with her own utter nothingness. The humility that is only ultimately learnt from experiencing 'he who is mighty doing great things', enabled her to be totally open to receive and be replenished with God's infinite goodness. She received all the infused virtues and gifts of the Holy Spirit, filling her and her family with the love of God and then, eventually, all families that would look to her for the motherly love and protection they craved.

Julian of Norwich makes this point clearly when she uses the example of Our Lady gazing upon God in profound mystical contemplation. 'The greatness and the nobility of this contemplation of God filled her full of reverent awe and with this she saw herself so humble and small, so simple and so poor in comparison with her Lord God that this reverent awe filled her with humility. And so, founded on this she was filled with grace and with every kind of virtue' (Long text, chapter 7).

We may think that all this may well be wonderful for Our Lady, who was immaculately conceived and free from the sin and selfishness that prevents us from turning to God, as she did, to be lost in mystical contemplation. But what about us? We fail to understand what this meant for her spiritual life. It meant as Simeon said in the Temple, that a sword of suffering would pierce her heart and that suffering would be multiplied many times over the sufferings of any other mother. All the great mystics who have arrived at the peak of the spiritual journey know, as Mary came to know and experience, what it means to have her human heart and soul totally possessed by divine love. It made heart and soul infinitely more open and sensitive to all the pain and suffering that she had to endure. It was bad enough when her motherly love saw and experienced every tiny twist and turn of suffering in her Son as he grew to maturity, but thereafter, it became all but unbearable.

From the very moment that he began to preach, the news of his preaching that was music to her ears was counterpointed by manic crescendos as the usual rabble of dissenters accused him of everything from heresy and perverting the people to being possessed by demonic powers. His arrival to speak in his own hometown should have been one of her greatest joys, but it turned out to be a nightmare when the rabble that was roused against him took him to the edge of a cliff to do away with him. The joy of his escape was only short-lived because she continued to hear the evil, seditious lies levied against him. She must have known

how it was going to end when St John the
Baptist (the man described by her Son as the
most saintly man who had ever lived) was
beheaded by the dissolute and debauched
King Herod for speaking the same truth that
her own Son was preaching. When the end
did come, and she stood at the foot of the
Cross, no heart before or since has been so
broken. No heart before or since has been
so delicate and so sensitive to the ultimate
powers of evil that were responsible for
the greatest and cruellest crime in human
history.

Just before he died, Jesus gave his mother,
Mary, to the loving care and compassion of
the apostle of love, St John. This gesture was
seen as having universal significance. This
divine action enabled her to be the mother
to the Church over which he presided while
she was on earth and also to be the mother
of us all after her glorious Assumption into
heaven. After this had taken place, time and

space no longer prevented her from being to all of us, in every time and place, the Mother she has been ever since and will continue to be in this world and the next.

Chapter 6

The Fruits of Contemplation

THERE ARE NO BETTER WORDS, nor a better way to describe what we must do on earth to bring about God's Kingdom of Love, than the words of St Thomas Aquinas. He said that the vocation of the Church, and of all who are privileged to belong to the Church, is 'To contemplate and to share the fruits of contemplation with others.' In his writings, it is quite clear that in saying this, he is not speaking so much about our ultimate destiny in heaven but our ultimate destiny here on earth.

This is the prayer that enabled Our Lady at all times to be able to fix her loving gaze upon God both before and after the glorification of her Son, Jesus. After her Son's glorification, however, her contemplation of God became far more powerful, far more intensive, and far more fruitful. This enhancement occurred because then, she not only prayed with her Son, as before, but in, with, and through him. What she received in return was God's love in ever greater measure than before, and contained within that love were all the infused virtues. It is to these infused virtues that we all aspire, together with all the other supernatural gifts, that expanded her motherhood more fully and more deeply than before.

St Peter was, without doubt, the rock upon which the Church was founded. But Mary, the Mother of God, was its mother to whom all would turn to discover in depth and in detail the life of Jesus, from his birth in a wooden crib to his death on a wooden cross. For this alone, the new fraternity that came to be called the Church was utterly unique. It was this personal and deeply emotional knowledge that became the spiritual lifeblood of the early Church. The first Apostles and disciples had their memories and their recollections, and while these close and fervent followers of Christ might well have been saints in the making, they were not saints yet. This would take many years of spiritual purification before they could contemplate their Lord as Mary did. Many people forget that a great apostle like St Paul, for instance, took ten years in spiritual preparation before he became the apostle to the Gentiles.

Her Immaculate Conception meant that Our Lady was totally free from the selfishness and sin and the sources of pride and prejudice that rule spiritual beginners. That is why Our Lady needed to remain behind after her Son returned to heaven. In the oldest and most ancient images or Icons of the first Pentecost day, it is always Our Lady who stands out pre-eminently, with the sign of the Holy Spirit's presence over her head. They all received the Holy Spirit simultaneously, but they all had to practise the repentance that St Peter preached for many years before the Holy Spirit did in them what he immediately did in Our Lady. Because of her Immaculate Conception, there was no sin or any remnants of sin in her to prevent the immediate action of the Holy Spirit. That is why the wisdom promised to all at the Last Supper instantly filled Our Lady to overflowing at the first Pentecost.

Many have wondered why Jesus wanted his mother to remain behind after his return to heaven. We can now see why. Whilst the others were being prepared and purified by the Holy Spirit, learning to contemplate and receive the fruits of contemplation as she had, she would remain behind. She would remain at the centre of the Church to do what her Son would have done if his life had not come to such a premature and ignominious end. The writing of the Gospels would be delayed until the evangelists were sufficiently purified by the Holy Spirit in prayer and thus enabled to receive his inspiration to write them. For, these precious works had to be written without injecting into them the pride or the prejudice that always distorts the truth in the works of purely secular writers, even those with the best will in the world. In this strange spiritual limbo land existent before the Holy Spirit could become fully effective in the Apostles through practising the repentance that St Peter preached, Our Lady stood out.

As the mother of the fledgling Church, her Immaculate Conception meant that she certainly knew more about her Son and his teaching than anyone else, yet there was something more. She embodied in her person and her personal sanctity all the infused virtues and gifts of the Holy Spirit that had not yet been fully developed in everyone else. The apostles spent years learning the practise of following Mary's example and thus allowing the Holy Spirit to work in them the way he had done in her. It was only after they mastered this teaching that God drew her up and into Heaven. Here, she was united with her Son to become the Queen of Heaven and Mother of the Universe. It was in those vital years before the Holy Spirit had fully established the Church as Jesus intended that Our Lady's role in its spiritual foundation was crucial. The first commandment was integrated into her daily prayer, as it was in the daily prayer of all the first Christians, most of whom would have been Jewish. In order to practise that prayer as God intended, they would have to learn how to love God by firstly learning to love him in Jesus Christ, her Son. Only Our Lady's recollection of him and what he said and did, as well as how he loved, was free of the pride and prejudice that would distort the recollection of others.

That is why it is to Our Lady, more than
to any other, to whom we are indebted for
teaching the early Church the way to the
contemplation that was her supreme prayer
then, as it still is now. The practice that,
above all others, would enable everyone
to come to know and love God by loving
him in Jesus Christ Our Lord was called
meditation. And it is as vital today as it
was in the early Church to lead sincere
believers into a loving relationship with
Christ that will eventually lead them on
and into mystical contemplation. It is this
sublime, supernatural prayer that all who
dwell in the mystical and glorified body of
Christ experience now, as they will eventually
experience it continually to all eternity in
heaven.

We may not have the inspired wisdom of
Our Lady to teach us in person as she taught
so many in the early Church, but we do
have on hand the sacred scriptures of the

New Testament. They were written by men who practised daily repentance and sacrifice in prayer, eventually enabling the Holy Spirit to inspire them to write them for us. Always remember that the scriptures were first written not for scholars to study and haggle over nor to prove their pet theological theses but, above all else, to love the only man who can bring about our personal salvation and the personal salvation of others.

The fruits of contemplation to which meditation finally leads are not given just for us but for others. Our Christian vocational calling is not merely for our salvation but for that of others; therefore, we must reconvert the world back to Christ. This cannot be done without the contemplation that fills us with the infused virtues and the gifts of the Holy Spirit. Be sure of this: they are given in their fullness only through the contemplation that was the daily prayer of Our Lady, who is now and forever Our Heavenly Queen and Mother.

CHAPTER 7

THE ROAD TO PERDITION

IF THE SUN became a symbol of God's
love shining in the risen Christ, then the
moon was a symbol of his mother, shining
with his reflected glory, even here on
earth, to lead all to union with her Son.
It was her contemplation and the fruits
of contemplation that shone in her that
inspired others to follow her in the only way
to union with God and the only way to lead
others to follow.

St Francis of Assisi once said there are two
ways of calling others to God. The first
and most important way is by embodying
his life in our own lives, which should be
replete with the virtues that characterised
his life. The second is by preaching, but
without the first way, the second way will

fail. The success of Christianity in those first centuries was that they followed the practical example and teaching of Mary in whom her Son's teaching and praying were so perfectly embodied. Centuries before religious life grew up, it was through the love of Christ learnt in prayer and meditation that found its fullest expression in contemplation. In this way, it was the infused virtues and gifts of the Holy Spirit that raised saints in abundance to transform a pagan Roman Empire into a Christian Roman Empire in such a short time.

When, at the end of the fifth century, the Catholic Emperor Theodosius made Christianity the official religion of the Roman Empire, things changed. The days were numbered for contemplation being the ultimate goal of the ordinary Christian family prayer, which Our Lady presided over. The ideal became ever more distant as the world, which Christians were called to change, instead changed them, and it changed them into its own image and likeness, not God's.

All that was once good and holy was all but changed into its opposite. The repentance originally meant to turn people to God now turned them inward upon themselves, to seek not God's own honour and glory but their own. Instead of the prayer that was meant to help them rise up to God, they began to rise in the world. Sacrifice that once meant making offerings to God now meant making offerings to man for material preferment. In subsequent centuries, there was always the remnant who kept the faith and from whom regular renewals arose. Perhaps it was from the time of Constantine that the graph that once charted the spiritual advancement of the Church upwards began to decline downward. Thanks to great saints like St Gregory, St Bernard, St Francis of Assisi and other magnificent saints and mystics, the steady downward trajectory of our spiritual graph made striking upward movements that were successful for a while. Repentance returned, the sacrifice that turned people back to prayer was made, and the liturgy that expressed these sacrifices once again reflected the vibrant life-changing celebrations that were commonplace in the early Church.

With the Renaissance that began in the middle of the fourteenth century, the birth of the man-centred modern world gradually began to seep into the Catholic Faith, infiltrating and finally strangling it into near death, as we can see today. But first, thanks to the council of Trent, there was a final flurry of spirituality and devotion culminating in the revival of a deep spirituality in which contemplation was once again seen as the ideal lived by Our Lady and practised as the culmination of the spiritual life by the first Christians. Once again, what St Thomas Aquinas called the fruits of contemplation made the seventeenth century the place where what had so often been lost and found in the past flourished again and gave hope of the return to our true spiritual origins. But sadly, the condemnation of a counterfeit mysticism called Quietism, riddled with heresy and the sins to which it led, set in motion anti-mystical witch hunts that have successfully outlawed mystical prayer and contemplation down to the present day. There has always been a remnant there to retain the essence of the faith that Jesus introduced into the early Church and over which Mary presided; however, the way of meditation that leads to and is culminated in contemplation was gone. At best, it was seen only as an extraordinary way for the few—the eccentric few. The thinking was akin to, 'God bless them, but don't dare follow them.'

Take love out of a family, and disaster follows. Take the God-given love that is given out of the Church, and the disasters that we have all seen will multiply as time plays out. With no one else to speak out and be heard, Our Lady has returned to centre stage to warn that even God's Mercy has its limits. Many believe it was Our Lady's frightening Fatima warnings regarding the impending consequences awaiting people who do not return to repentance, prayer, and sacrifice that galvanised Pope John to call a council to prevent the horrors contained in the so-called 'Fatima Secret'. If this were indeed the impetus leading the pope to attempt to direct his flock to safer pastures, then it failed. It failed because it neglected to reproduce a document that would inspire us all to return to the profound God-given spirituality that Jesus Christ introduced into the early Church.

I personally believe that this is the greatest tragedy of modern times, not just for the Church but for the world. It did produce a document that set before the faithful a modern version of the ancient liturgy in which the early Christians expressed their faith. That was well and good, but without the profound contemplative spirituality born of repentance, prayer, and sacrifice over which Our Lady presided for a time, it would mean little. What is a beautiful liturgical expression of the faith without the presence of the faithful who daily live and practise the spirituality of repentance, prayer, and sacrifice?

In the years that have followed, everything has become progressively worse as people have turned to the latest human wisdom to make up for the divine wisdom that they have been denied. They seem to believe—and wrongly believe—that they can do for themselves what only the divine wisdom received in contemplation can do for them.

Chapter 8

Our Lady of Mount Carmel

WHEN MARY CALLED HERSELF 'Our Lady of Mount Carmel' in her appearances, she was teaching us something extremely profound. She wanted to identify herself with the contemplative spirituality contained in the teaching of the Carmelite orders, who chose her as their patroness. It is a reminder that we should pursue contemplation as our ultimate spiritual destiny and that our spirituality should be primarily directed toward the supreme form of prayer that Our Lady practised throughout her life.

The place where this vocation is pursued is in the world, but more precisely in the family, for this is the place in which Christianity was first born. It grew and flourished three hundred years before St Antony founded a monastic community in the Egyptian desert. It was also a thousand years or more before the Franciscans, Dominicans, and Augustinian friars were founded, and the Carmelite Simon Stock was given the brown scapular by Our Lady. In the first years of Christianity, the glorious and most spiritually productive years in its history, it was the family that was the wellspring and source of authentic Catholic spirituality that transformed the world. Apostolic religious orders would come later, but they were primarily trying to perform a rear-guard action. They were trying to retrieve and bring back the vital family-based faith that was once, and still could be now, the heart and soul of the sublime faith that Jesus Christ introduced into the early Church.

In ancient times, the family was the place where children learnt of and were inspired by their illustrious ancestors. In the evenings, the fireside or the hearth was the place where their parents, their elders, and even professional storytellers would relate tales of their origins and the great heroes of the past. It was here that great books like the Iliad, the Odyssey and the Bible were first heard while endlessly and lovingly retold. Unaffected by phenomena like the mass media, memories were extremely sharp and retentive. Volumes would be retained in the memory to inspire those who lived in the present and to inspire those who were to be born in the future.

This is how and where Our Lady would have learnt and then handed on ancient traditions to her own family and to the Son, who would become the source of a new and far more dramatic tradition, which would, in its turn, be handed on to others. Mary, our Mother, was, above and beyond all others, the living embodiment of that new tradition that she endlessly pondered and reflected upon. It was a tradition that began even before her

Son, Jesus, was born and continued even after his death and Resurrection. It was to her, more than to any other, that all would turn to hear this new tradition that so perfectly fulfilled the older tradition with its prophecies and promises—all of which found their ultimate completion in her Son, the fruit of her womb.

She was not only the inspiration for the Gospels, when much of this tradition was written down, but even before they were written. This would, in its turn, lead to a deep and personal embodiment of this new tradition in people's hearts and minds. Here, as Mary did herself, others would be taught to ponder over all that she and the other Apostles had taught them. After they practised the daily prayer they inherited from their Jewish ancestors, albeit Christianised, to reflect their new presence in Christ's Mystical Body, they would practise meditation. For this new means of prayer called meditation, they had their Mother Mary to thank more than any other.

Although Mary did continue to ponder over the events of her life and her love for Jesus, her Son, her prayer was at first different to all others. Now that she had been swept up into her Son's Mystical Body, she not only prayed with him but in, with and through him in a remarkably sublime way. In this prayer, her own sacred and Immaculate Heart was suffused with his to be united in a profound act of love. In this transcendent act of divine loving, her heart and his Sacred Heart were suffused together as one in contemplating the infinite glory of God. Here, with her Son, Mary would experience what St Paul called 'the height and depth the length and breadth of the love that surpasses all understanding' (Ephesians 3:18). She would be drawn for a time, even in this world, into the ecstatic bliss that would for a brief time enable her to experience what she would experience for all time when she was assumed into heaven and enthroned as Queen of Heaven and Mother to all.

What mother, after experiencing such supernatural bliss, would not want to share what she has experienced with her children? Knowing that love would enable them to enjoy the mystical contemplation that she had experienced, she encouraged and inspired all to come to know and love her Son, firstly, as she had known and loved him on earth. That is why she relentlessly persuaded everyone to pursue daily meditation on the life of the most mature, perfect, and lovable person who has ever walked on the face of this world. She knew that, as this love grew through daily meditation, the love that was generated would begin to desire to be united with the one who was loved.

Although you can come to know and love someone who is dead, you cannot be united with them as you might wish. That is why, at this point in the spiritual journey, for those who have persevered in meditation, the Holy Spirit leads us into a new form of prayer called purifying contemplation, where we will be prepared and purified to be united with her Son. Because Mary was Immaculately conceived, the supreme prayer of contemplation was as natural to her as giving birth to the Son of God, thanks to the Holy Spirit. But for those of us who would follow her, it means listening more carefully to her message and putting it into practice in our daily lives.

Chapter 9

Listening to the Message

WE HAVE ALREADY SEEN that Our Lady's call to repentance simply means that she is asking us to return to what we have long since forgotten. Her call is to keep turning back to God. Prayer is the word she used to describe how this change in our life can best be brought about. In her own life, she practised daily formal prayers taught by her own parents that were Christianised after her Son, Jesus, was glorified. This helped her prepare to sanctify her day in such a way that she could keep turning to God in all she said and did through all whom she served and loved.

Then, there is another form of prayer to which she could turn at any moment of the day when she was working or travelling because it was so simple. That prayer, as we have seen, is called contemplation. I will shortly be showing the steps we can take to be drawn up into this sublime prayer through the style of meditation she inspired others to practise. The sacrifices she calls for are not the self-sought sacrifices performed to demonstrate how spiritually strong we are but the sacrifices that show that we realise just how weak we are. That is because they are all primarily made to help us keep turning to God in prayer, to enable us to keep loving him always.

If, at first, these sacrifices do not seem all that difficult, we must not get ahead of ourselves trying to show how we can do great things for God before he has given us the grace to do so. The meditation Mary helped to encourage and inspire in the early Church will soon bear fruit if we regularly persevere long enough. This practice of trying to love God— made flesh and blood in her Son, Jesus—will come to a natural climax. We will reach this peak when our desire to love God has been sufficiently manifested by our daily constant endeavour. Taking us at our word, as it were, God sends his Holy Spirit to lead us into the beginning of a new form of prayer, which Our Lady knew and practised, that came to be called mystical contemplation.

This prayer came naturally to Our Lady because she was immaculately conceived. We, however, are not because sin and self-absorption prevent us from experiencing the love that she experienced at all times. Before we can practise the sublime contemplation that she practised, all the sin and selfishness in us that prevent us from doing this must be purified. This takes not years but decades in the best of us, and it is, at times, not at all pleasant. But without purification, how can we possibly expect our unpurified hearts to be united with the Sacred Hearts of Jesus and Mary?

Now, we will be asked to sacrifice our time and give up the pleasures and the pastimes that prevent us from giving our all, our energy, and our love to God. These sacrifices, made in trying to love God in prayer and trying to love God in the neighbour in need, beginning in our own homes, are the sacrifices that are offered to God through Our Lord Jesus when we go to Mass. Here, as we offer our humble sacrifices with those of others to God—in, with, and through the sacrifice of Our Risen Lord—something life-transforming happens. He returns the sacrifices we offer a hundredfold with his love. This enables us to continue to serve him in the forthcoming week, reinvigorated with his love and surcharged with the power of his Holy Spirit.

This will not only enable us to keep the first commandment with ever greater verve and vigour but the second of the two new commandments, too: that is, to love our neighbour as Christ himself loves us. Thus, the four simple counsels that Our Lady asks of us sum up the essence of the Gospel spirituality and the spirituality practised in the early Church that can still do for the modern world what it did for the ancient world. But only if we learn the simple message that Our Lady has been relentlessly giving to save the world from the disasters that prolonged human selfishness will finally do to it.

If someone held a knife to your throat or threatened to blow up your home unless you promised to repent and change your life, what would you say? Anybody can promise to do anything when threatened with death, but that is quite a different thing from persevering once the threat is taken away. Now is the time to do of our own free will and our own volition what the Christ who died for us asks of us. Namely, to love him in return and to enable him to give us not only true and abiding happiness in this life but ongoing and ever-increasing happiness and love in the next, together with all we love and hold dear.

If we act under extreme pressure to do what we have long since forgotten, it is certainly better than not acting at all. Yet, if we freely act now of our own free will, we will not only save ourselves from what is to come but others, too, who will meet the loving God again in us. That is because our prayer has enabled us to be filled with the love of God and all the infused virtues and gifts of the Holy Spirit, which enable us to do all things possible—even the impossible.

If we are indeed residing in the last minute of extra time, why wait a moment longer? What I am writing will show you how to start again, beginning now!

Chapter 10

The Rosary

ST PAUL CALLED the wondrous divine plan, sharing the glory and joy of heaven with everyone, the Mysterion. In English, this is translated as 'God's Secret plan' from the Greek word meaning secret, hidden or invisible. Throughout history, even Jewish history, this plan remained a secret, although the Jews believed that when God's special envoy—the Messiah—arrived, all would be revealed. When the Messiah did arrive as promised, he explained God's Plan but told them that only those who radically changed their lives and continually changed them would be qualified to enter into this new world that he called the 'Kingdom of God'. Knowing that human beings are weak, after he departed from this world, he promised to send his love—his Holy Spirit—to surcharge weak human love with divine love to help make the journey to heavenly bliss possible. The first to receive his Holy Spirit was his own mother, Mary, together with the first Apostles and three thousand others on the first Pentecost day.

Mary and the Apostles were immediately drawn up and into the Mystical Body of Christ where, in future, together with all who through baptism would join them, they would begin their journey into what both Jesus and St Paul called Paradise. Because of her Immaculate Conception, Mary would immediately be united with and become as one with the dear Son to whom she had given birth. Her contemplation would now be as one with his contemplation as they would together gaze upon and be enthralled by the glory of the One whom Jesus said was their divine and loving Dad.

Until the Apostles were ready and prepared, Mary would stay on in this world before joining her Son in glory. While on earth, Jesus was the flesh and blood embodiment of God's plan here on earth. That is why he was the world's first true mystic. In other words, he was not only at all times open to receiving the inner mystical life and love of God, but he was able to transmit it to others, and after his death, he continued to do this. The Apostles would become mystics, too, when, after continual repentance, the love of Jesus that was poured upon them began to reside within them and began to overflow onto and into all who met them. The first priests, then, were mystics, as all priests are meant to be. They were not only empowered to administer what were then called the mysteries, or later the sacraments, to others but to continually support and guide individuals on their journey in Christ to reach the paradise for which he had prepared them.

All priests to the end of time are expected to become mystics to do this work, as were the first Apostles who were mystics before them. They are all called—and this is their vocation—to come to know and experience for themselves that love to which they are called to guide others. If the reader is bemused by what I am saying, then it is a clear sign of just how far we have veered from the implementing God's plan as he originally conceived it. It is a sad and deplorable state of affairs if those people ordained to implement the mysteries, now called the sacraments, to sanctify and make holy those who receive them are not mystics.

By mystics, I mean men whose whole lives are dedicated to receiving for themselves the inner hidden or mystical inner life and love of God. Men, therefore, whose whole formation is primarily orientated from the first day to this end, long before the requisite intellectual knowledge deemed necessary is introduced. That is why there should be a novitiate for secular as well as religious priests so that, when formal intellectual learning begins, it should be learnt together with the practice of the spiritual life to which they have already been introduced in a novitiate. This is the best possible way to ensure that the faithful have good and holy priests to guide them. This also enables those with no aptitude for what matters most to be sent away.

Our Lady never used the Rosary herself while she was on earth, neither did the Apostles, later saints, or any of the faithful for over a thousand years because the prayer had not yet been devised. It is, nevertheless, the prayer that she has constantly recommended to those to whom she has appeared in recent years. Even though this new means of prayer is not a sacrament, it can be called a sacramental because it can do today what the first mysteries did for the early Christians for whom she was a mother. That is why they are called the mysteries of the Rosary because by saying them and meditating upon them, they can generate the love in us that enables us to enter ever more deeply into the Mysterion—God's plan for us made flesh and blood in the glorified body of Our Risen Lord, Jesus Christ.

This prayer contains within it the way to all prayer, and that is why Our Lady calls upon us all to use it. It may seem, to begin with, that it is purely devised to encourage vocal prayer, but that would be only a superficial understanding of this prayer. Practitioners who, through the Hail Mary, relentlessly call upon Our Lady to pray for them will be led by the same Holy Spirit who conceived Christ in her and into the meditation that leads to contemplation. Here, they will experience the supreme prayer that was the daily prayer of Our Lady herself. This is the prayer that finally enabled her Sacred Heart to be united to the Sacred Heart of Jesus, even in this life, as it can do for us if we only follow her example.

For me, one of the wonders of the Rosary is that it can lead the simplest and humblest of souls to the heights of mystical union without them ever realising it. This prayer was the prayer par excellence after the heresy of Quietism had deprived the vast majority of religious and ordinary faithful of the profound mystical contemplation that had always been the heart and soul of its inner prayer life from the very beginning. The censors, who were always looking to trod upon and destroy any sort of prayer that had the slightest whiff of Quietism, considered the Rosary harmless and, therefore, commendable. But for the person who uses it as intended, it can be the most revolutionary of all prayers because it can lead those committed to it, as Our Lady intended, into the sort of meditation she both encouraged and made possible in the early Church. Thence, from meditation to contemplation.

When I used to visit my mother at the end of her life, she lay in bed holding her Rosary, and she said that she could no longer use it as she once did. It was enough to hold it in her hands as she said the Holy Name or some other simple prayer before lapsing into moments of contemplative stillness. It was then that my mother joined Mary in the prayer that she said on earth and still says in heaven.

I will now turn to each of the mysteries to offer a few words to help lead a beginner into meditation. This is the meditation that Our Lady, more than any other, presided over in the early Church, and the Holy Spirit will then lead the believer where he will. It may be ideal to say the whole of the Rosary when it is said in common, but when said alone, just one decade may be enough if it is said slowly and prayerfully and meditated upon with deep, loving affection and prayerful reactions as long as the Holy Spirit determines. That is more than enough until he leads you onward in whatever way he wishes.

Chapter 11

The Joyful Mysteries

1. The Annunciation

AT THE VERY BEGINNING, before time began, the infinite goodness of God burnt with a desire to share with others the ecstatic bliss of being alive, enveloped in love beyond measure from and to all eternity. A new world would have to be created in a new dimension of space and time, in which new beings would be created in his own image and likeness. They would be made of flesh and blood to inherit the glorious destiny that God wanted them to enjoy, with Him and in Him. This new world would be created in the beginning. As St John in his initial gospel chapter puts it, 'All things were created in the Word and the Word was made flesh'. This Incarnate Word would, in the fullness of time, be born into this world to be its King, clothed in flesh and blood like those born before and after him. If this plan depended on a King of flesh and blood, then he must be born of a perfect human mother or, to be more precise, a perfect human Queen.

Therefore, Mary was conceived from before time began as an Immaculate Mother. Like all other human beings who preceded her, she was made free to love or not to love. Thus, even God's infinite love would have to depend on her freely choosing to receive it. When she said 'yes', time seemed to stand still; even eternity held its breath. If only it was known, the whole of humankind—already born and yet to be born—would have exploded with joy. All the musicians that ever were, all the voices that had been and were yet to come, would orchestrate a glorious rendering of the Te Deum to give thanks to God. They would also give thanks to Mary and the Son that her loving fiat would bring into the world to inaugurate a timeless and heavenly destiny for all who would receive him. After meditating on this, the first mystery of the rosary, it is time to offer our thanks, our gratitude to God, and to the one who said 'yes' to make his plans for us come true.

2. The Visitation

Someone other than Mary might have broadcast her good fortune to the world or at least told the news she had just received to the women in her village. Who would have blamed her if she had set out immediately for Jerusalem to tell the great and the good that 'he who is mighty had done great things' in her? As a direct descendent of King David who was to give birth to his heir—another King, the Messiah—she would have been garlanded with glory. Who would have been surprised if a new Palace was to be built in her honour for her to reside in with her husband Joseph, also of the line of David?

However, instead of rushing off to Jerusalem to be feted by the High Priest and his entourage, she rushed off to visit and serve her elderly cousin, Elizabeth, who had also been told by the angel Gabriel that she would give birth to a child. After humbly preparing Elizabeth to give birth to John the Baptist—the man who would herald the coming of her Son and his Kingdom—she came back home, without any fuss, to prepare for the birth of the King of Kings in all humility and without any of the prestige that such an event merited.

3. The Birth of Our Lord in the Stable at Bethlehem

Whatever the circumstances that led to Mary giving birth in Bethlehem, it had been long since decided by God because Bethlehem was the ancestral home of the illustrious human ancestor of Jesus, King David. However, it was more man's selfishness and thoughtlessness than God's planning that his divine Son should be born in a stable without any pomp or ceremony, laid not in a cradle but a manger made for cattle to feed from. It may or may not have been warm enough to give birth in, but the place must have held the stench of all stables and been open to all passers-by to gawp at the pitiful sight of a young mother giving birth to her beloved Son in abject poverty.

Regardless, angels did sing, and shepherds did come to see and give glory to the man born to be King, not just of their world but of the whole world that was made for him. The only other royalty to come were three kings from the East. The only king from the West wanted to murder him for daring to threaten his Kingdom. While Herod was planning to murder all other young babies in the vicinity to make sure none should rival him, the new family had to flee into Egypt like unwanted immigrants. Thus began the life of Jesus Christ, Our Lord and Saviour, who, after being placed in a wooden manger, began a life that would end on a wooden cross outside Jerusalem. Nevertheless, it is time to give thanks to God with the shepherds for what happened on that day and for every day in the future for those with hearts open to receive him.

4. The Presentation in the Temple

After the terrible slaughter of the innocents, Jesus, Mary, and Joseph returned from exile in time for the presentation of Jesus in the Temple. It was Jewish custom for parents to offer their firstborn to God and make a sacrifice in thanksgiving. Surely, the Holy Family anticipated the joy of this event;

however, they became shrouded in sorrow after encountering a devout and holy man called Simeon. At first, all went well. Taking the child in his arms. he gave thanks to God that he had lived to see and hold the Messiah, who was not only destined to be the glory to Israel but to the whole world, whom he would enlighten with the truth. However, Simeon was further inspired by the Holy Spirit to reveal that the child would be rejected by many who should have received him and, furthermore, that his own dear mother's heart would be pierced by the sword of suffering.

Apart from the circumstance of her Son's birth, Mary had enjoyed a comparatively carefree life, but things would change. She would see the Son she loved and cherished hated and despised by those who should have welcomed him. When her pride was overflowing while he came to preach in their own home, Nazareth, she heard the crowds condemning him as a mountebank and blasphemer, and, had it not been for a miracle, he would have been put to death.

Who will ever know the indescribable horrors Mary went through to see her Son tortured and crucified to death? Who will ever know the nightmares she suffered before she was assumed into heaven? All this was part of our salvation, for which we must ever be indebted to and thankful to the Mother, who will always understand and love us, no matter what. No suffering we will ever be asked to bear will ever rival hers, nor, therefore, the loving understanding that is always ours for the asking.

5. The finding in the Temple

Imagine what suffering she must have gone through when it seemed her own Son, the Messiah, the boy destined to be King of Israel and all humanity, was lost for three days at the age of only twelve. Had he been taken and eaten by wild beasts on the journey home, killed by robbers, or taken by slavers? Or perhaps, knowing who he was and the threat that he may be to the establishment, some latter-day Herod had quietly eliminated him. All turned out well when he was discovered discussing the scriptures in the Temple and astounding his listeners with his intelligence.

When, understandably, his parents remonstrated with him, he gave a puzzling reply, which in modern English was, 'I was here all the time! Did you not know where I would have been?' Although the family always came to Jerusalem to celebrate the feast of Passover, it was the first time Jesus was old enough to meet with and question expert scripture scholars. It would have enabled him to find out more about his illustrious forebears, about the Kings from whom he had descended, and the prophets who had already foretold his great destiny to which he was called and his determined death.

His behaviour was not that of an impetuous, self-willed boy but of a young man born to be king, enthralled by listening to doctors and scholars speaking about God's plans for him and thus losing all sense of time. That this was a single event, a moment of understandable forgetfulness, is made plain by the last words in the second Chapter of St Luke:

'He went down with them to Nazareth where he lived under their authority.'

Chapter 12

The Luminous mysteries

1. The Baptism of Christ by John the Baptist

WHEN A CHRISTIAN KING IS CROWNED, he is invested with power by God himself through the Holy Spirit, whose presence is symbolised by the sacred anointing. The Baptism of Christ in the River Jordan by John the Baptist was Christ's coronation on earth. The Father of Christ expressed his pride in being there with the words, 'This is my beloved Son in whom I am well pleased' (Matthew 3:17). It was not oil but a Dove of Peace that represented the Holy Spirit, who invested Christ with the Father's power. Here, it was made clear that his Kingdom on earth was unlike any other kingdom, which would be a reign of Peace.

Christ himself made it quite clear from the outset that, although he came as the Lord of Lords and the King of Kings, he did not come to lord it over anyone but to serve. The service he came to deliver was the most perfect form of service that one person could perform for another human being. That service was offered to all who would receive it to the fullness of the love of God from whom all love comes. From the moment Christ began to preach, he showed clearly that this is the service he came to perform for all who are prepared to radically change their lives. This is the service he offered to change us all beyond our wildest hopes and dreams.

2. The Marriage Feast at Cana

It may have been expected that Christ the King would immediately begin proclaiming that his Kingdom had now come or was close at hand. Instead, he went to a wedding feast in Cana, where he again met up with his beloved mother and performed the first of his many miracles. What might seem a random whim was a well-prepared part of his plan to set up his Kingdom on earth. Whereas other later great kingdoms would be ruled by Kings, primarily through a great and powerful oligarchy of wealthy Dukes, Earls, and Barons, Christ's Kingdom would be ruled by the family that would be the heart and soul of his new Kingdom. God had already put the family in pride of place in the Old Testament, and now Christ would do the same in the New Testament. Hence, his visit to Cana in Galilee. It was at his mother's behest that what was called a miracle took place, but which St John in his gospel calls a sign. The change of water into wine—ostensibly, an act of kindness and compassion—was the hallmark of all Christ's later miracles and had, like most of them, a deeper or spiritual meaning.

Compared to marriage, which was the heart and soul of Jewish spirituality, the new marriages in the new Christian spirituality would be as different as water from wine. It would be far more powerful and dynamic because human love would, in this sacrament, enable God to suffuse and surcharge human love with divine love. In this way, grace would build on what was primarily human love to convert it into divine love. The married couple who are the ministers of this transformed human love would share this love with one another not just on their wedding day but on every day. This love would then overflow onto their children as the new inheritors of Christ's new Kingdom of Love and Peace.

3. The Proclamation of the Kingdom

At first sight, it may be thought that, after the Marriage feast at Cana, Christ began to preach that the Kingdom had come.

That would not be quite true, although, admittedly, there is some ambivalence. At his baptism in the Jordan, the Kingdom had come in him as he was invested with full power by the Holy Spirit. However, the Kingdom had not yet come fully for others to whom he preached. Note his words that the Kingdom is coming, is at hand, but not that the Kingdom has come for all. It was when Christ was celebrating with his disciples the feast of the Tabernacles, which recalled the long sojourn of the Jews in the desert, that this point is made clear by St John in his Gospel. During the ceremony celebrating the moment when Moses struck a rock from which water flowed to slake the thirst of his people, a text from Isaiah was read. It promised that when the Messiah came, he would slake the spiritual thirst of his people with none other than the Holy Spirit.

Lest there was any misunderstanding, St John added a sentence specifying that the

Holy Spirit had not yet been sent, although it was obvious to all his disciples that the Messiah had come. The Holy Spirit had come and was present on earth in Christ himself after his coronation on earth, but it would only be poured out on everyone after his coronation in heaven on the first Pentecost day. While on earth, therefore, Christ proclaimed only that God's Kingdom was coming but not that it had fully come for all. Before this happened, his work on earth was to prepare those who would repent because, when the time came, only those who would repent continually would be admitted into his Kingdom of Love and Peace.

4. The Transfiguration

Before Jesus left this world, he wanted to show his closest Apostles—Peter, James, and John—what it would be like for all, not just on earth after the Holy Spirit had been sent but after they died and joined him in heaven. He did this on the top of Mount Tabor, where he was joined by Moses and Elijah to give his close friends a premonition of the future by showing what would happen to him after he had been glorified. What is immediately evident is that Jesus was telling them that, just as his body would be glorified and not just transformed into some form of supernatural spirit in heaven, so, too, their bodies would likewise be glorified.

This, of course, means that what Christ promised would happen to his apostles will happen to all of us who are true to him till death. After death, then, we will be united with all our loved ones—our fathers, mothers, husbands, wives, and children—not just in some pantheistic oneness, where our spirits are united with the spirit of God in an intangible, disembodied heaven. Now, we will be united with them, both spiritually and physically, to continually participate with them in a never-ending journey into the infinite love of God, in, with, and through Jesus Christ, our Risen and Glorified Lord.

5. The Last Supper

Despite their protestations to the contrary, after his Transfiguration, Jesus began to tell his disciples that the end was in sight and that his time had almost come. When his 'hour' was finally upon him, he sent ahead two of his apostles to prepare for the last Passover meal that he would share with them. The fact that his time had come even more swiftly than even he expected is indicated by the sheer amount of profound mystical teaching that he concentrated in summary form and gave to his Apostles at one sitting. Read what Jesus said, and read it over and over again to find and absorb ever more fully its sublime meaning each time you read it. It is the most sublime mystical teaching ever given.

This Last Supper—an even more sacred and holy sacrificial meal than that inaugurated by Moses when the paschal lamb, 'the lamb of God,' sacrificed in the Temple was eaten—would be celebrated by Jesus for the first time. The man John the Baptist called the Lamb of God took ordinary bread and wine into his holy and venerable hands. He blessed them and said for the first time those holiest of all words that transformed the ordinary bread and wine into his own body and blood. As if it were not enough that the Son of God should be made flesh and blood to live amongst us and teach us the mysteries that would enable us to follow him into heaven, he did something that is still too unbelievable for many to comprehend: he became present under the appearances of bread and wine. And for what purpose? It was not just so that he could, as he promised, make his home in us and enable us to make our home in him, but even more. It was to nourish and give us the inner power and strength to follow and put into practice his entire teaching. In meeting others, they would see in us the one who continues to work in and through us to bring to this world God's Kingdom of Love and of Peace 'as it is in heaven'.

Then, finally, this sacred spiritual food will sustain us to continue our journey to our final destiny. And this will take place in, with, and through Christ's own Mystical Body as we offer daily our little sacrifices to be joined with his. He continues to do now in heaven what he did on earth whilst continuing to perform the greatest act of loving self-sacrifice the world has ever known, upon which we must meditate next: the sorrowful mysteries.

Chapter 13

The Sorrowful Mysteries

1. The Agony in the Garden

FOR THE FIRST TIME, we see Our Lord at his most vulnerable. And things are about to get worse—so bad that what he is about to suffer is totally unimaginable. However, it is imaginable to him as he goes to pray with his closest friends in the Garden of Gethsemane for the help and strength he needs. He prays for all his worth as the full horror of what is about to take place presses upon him. Although his divine nature makes what is about to happen infinitely more horrifying, his human nature begins to rebel. It rebels against what he knows he must do, his Father's will. Almost involuntarily, he implores his Father to take away what is to happen to him in the day ahead. 'Father, that this chalice may be taken away from me', he prays over and over again. Then, drawing all his strength from the very depth of his being, he does what he knows is right and what he must do. He prays, 'But not my will be done, but your will be done' (Luke 22:42). Yet, is it God's will that he should suffer so much and so ignominiously? The truth is that it is not God's will but man's will.

All he did was preach the new Kingdom of Love, of goodness, peace, and justice. Nonetheless, this means condemning the world into which he was born, where these virtues were nowhere to be found, and their very opposites praised by those who now wished to destroy him. His sheer unalloyed goodness was a mirror that highlighted their badness, and now, they were to get their revenge. He will shortly send out his disciples to preach what he had preached. Can he use all his supernatural powers to avoid the consequences of bearing witness to the truth that they will have to suffer?

2. The Scourging at the Pillar

How would Our Lady have felt when she heard the terrible news of his condemnation to death? How could she have sufficiently controlled herself to go out to be as close to his side as possible to support him? She knew what would immediately follow the condemnation. The beautiful, loving baby she held, cuddled and kissed so many times, and with love the world had never before known would be torn to pieces with terrible scourges. These scourges were far worse than the whippings used to chastise common criminals. The instruments used were rather like the cat-o'-nine-tails used aboard ships; attached to each terrible tail were pieces of jagged bones, bits of metal, and even iron hooks. The purpose was not just to inflict excruciating pain but to rip out the flesh of the victim until he was more dead than alive once the scourging was done.

The damage done to the human frame was so devastating that Roman law ordered that a person should receive no more than forty lashes. This was not because there was the slightest sympathy for the sufferer but for fear that the ordeal would be such that the 'criminal' might die before their crucifixion. This was one of, if not the most ignominious deaths that the human mind has ever devised. Remember that Jesus had already told his followers, who sought to defend him upon his capture, that if he chose, he could have twelve legions of angels extinguish the excruciating agony he was suffering and thrust his tormenters into the bowels of hell.

The fact that he did not use his divine power at any point of his ordeal shows more courage, more strength, and more heroism than shown by the collective courage of all mankind since the world was created. This is the quality of the love that redeemed the world and can redeem each one of us personally. That is why, despite our understandable reluctance to do so, Our Lady has encouraged us to meditate on the quality of our Redeemer's love for us expressed in such a horrific way.

3. The crowning with thorns

When the lowest members of military life were chosen to scourge and crucify Jesus to death, they had heard enough of the conversation to set their evil imaginations alight. So, he thought he was a King? Pilate would put a plaque on the Cross to that effect, and his friends would worship him as a misunderstood deity who would rule them from some other world. Galvanised by the wine typically given to dull the conscience of the torturers, they decided to have a little sport. They dressed Christ in the purple cloak that King Herod had dressed him in. Then they crushed a crown of briars into his head and bowed before him in mock homage to his royal majesty.

Here was the King conceived by God before the world was created, the one in whom that world was made and who would, before the day was done, be crowned King of Heaven and Earth from the beginning to the end of time. Now, however, he was reduced to utter humiliation by a drunken rabble. Yet, before the hour was out, he would be praying to his Father for them to be forgiven because 'they know not what they do' (Luke 23:34). In this squalid little scene that has haunted the hearts and minds of saints for centuries, those with eyes to see can recognize the height and depth, the length and breadth of the love that was in the process of saving the world. Praised be Jesus Christ our King, and long may we serve him, giving love for love to the best of our abilities.

4. The Carrying of the Cross

According to St Padre Pio, a dislocated shoulder caused untold agony to Jesus, giving him severe pain and anguish whilst he was carrying his cross. It was this that forced the Roman executioners to make a visiting foreigner carry the Cross behind Jesus. If only Jesus had not entered the city the week before on a donkey but rather on a war horse flanked by ten thousand well-armed and highly trained troops. This would have enabled him to vanquish their oppressors and make Jerusalem, rather than Rome, the centre of the Empire. But he did not; therefore, the same people who had cheered his entry into Jerusalem now booed and jeered him on his way to be crucified.

Despite his faltering and forlorn state, he still had time to console the women of Jerusalem who had come to console him: 'Weep not for me, but for yourselves and for your children' (Luke 23:28). When you pause to meditate upon Christ's outrageous suffering, do not merely try to picture the scene in your imagination. Imagine that you were there. Witness Jesus as he is being condemned to death. Look upon him from behind a pillar as he is being scourged nearly to death. Observe the comtemptible charade enacted by the soldiers as Jesus is mocked for his outrageous pretensions. Scuffle amongst the jeering crowd as he stutters and stumbles his way to Calvary, and then take up your place beside John and Mary and with the other women and the disciples who did not run away but stayed to the end.

Keep your eyes open, watching and hearing everything. Then, open your mouth and speak to the One who is giving his all for you. This is how meditation enables our love to well up from within and to express the inexpressible as we try to offer our thanks, our love, and the promises of a changed life in which our ongoing love can give thanks to the most lovable and the most adorable man who ever lived.

5. The Crucifixion

Do not shrink from doing what many others did. Stay with Jesus in your imagination, with open hearts and minds. Do not be afraid to express your feelings as you gaze upon the greatest act of human loving that the world has ever known. See the drunken executioners hammer nails into his hands and feet. Then, hear him forgiving them as he will always forgive you, no matter how low you fall.

Listen to the roaring thunder, feel the rumbling earth and the splitting rock, and see the enshrouding darkness cover the whole world. Hear Christ speak to promise Paradise to the good thief, to commend his mother to the care of St John and him to her motherly love. Then, witness him as he falls into an unfathomable inner darkness as the end draws near. Hear those fighting words: 'My God, my God, why have you forsaken me?' (Matthew 27:46). Watch him endlessly trying to push his body upward for breath with his feet fastened with nails to the Cross on which he is dying in unprecedented anguish and inexpressible agony. Then, listen as he loudly cries out for all to hear those unforgettable words. 'It is completed' (John 19:30).

It is not just the agony that is completed, but all his work on earth that his Father sent him to set up the Kingdom that is soon to come. Now, at last, you can take heart, for you know with absolute certainty what many standing around the Cross do not know.

Christ is already in heaven with the good thief, whom he very recently pardoned and promised Paradise. But now, realise at the end of this exacting meditation that because of what happened on that day, Christ is close to you now in his risen glory—now and on every day—to fill you with the same love he poured out on the first Pentecost day.

Now is the time for a final thank you and a promise of a lifetime of thanks, not just in words but in what you do daily for the One who has given and continues to give his all for you and to all who are open to receive him. Praise be Jesus Christ our King!

CHAPTER 14

THE GLORIOUS MYSTERIES

1. The Resurrection

IT IS IRONIC that the first witnesses to the Resurrection were soldiers, some of whom could have been his torturers. They were so overwhelmed by what they saw that the whole world would soon know what they had seen and heard. Even more ironic was that the second group of people to be witnesses to the Resurrection were the leading priests and the Pharisees who had ordered his death in the first place. They so believed the soldiers that they paid large sums of money to keep them quiet. The soldiers were to say they had fallen asleep and that Jesus' wily disciples had hidden him in the night so as to deceive people into believing that he had risen from the dead.

Irrefutable evidence finally did convince all the disciples, as well as the doubters, that Jesus had indeed risen from the dead. It was not just that they saw the empty tomb and his shroud but that they saw Jesus himself. They saw him eat with them. They witnessed him working miracles again. They even touched him to prove he was not a figment of their hopeful imagination. Thomas actually put his hand into Jesus' speared side and his fingers into his nail-pierced hands. But, most of all, they listened to him speak and explain something that had not been explained before. He told them that if they had known the scriptures as well as they should have, it would have been expected that he must first suffer before entering into his glory.

Later, with hindsight, they would realise that he was not just telling them what was expected of him but what would be expected of those who would follow him if they tried to live and preach the same good news that he preached. Every one of Christ's followers may not be asked to carry a physical cross as he did. But they would have to carry a cross nevertheless, whilst daily dying to self because self-centred, arrogant human beings could not be his disciples. To represent him, they would have to become one with him to share in the fruits of his Resurrection.

From the very start, then, Christ called everyone who would follow him to take up their daily cross. No cross, no resurrection.

2. The Ascension

Before he ascended into heaven forty days after the Resurrection, Jesus told the one hundred and forty disciples who came to say farewell that they were to go out baptising all peoples in his name. Furthermore, they would have to teach the new converts all he had taught them. Nor were they to be surprised, for as he warned them at the Last Supper, those who lived in the shadow land do not take kindly to being shown the light. Truth is not a dainty dish to be set before the world's most dangerous animals, especially if they have political or religious pretensions. If you persist in teaching it to those who do not want to hear it, beware. They can become very cross, and they can crucify, as the disciples had recently experienced this frightening lesson for themselves! But it was not all doom and gloom because, as Jesus also told the disciples at the Last Supper, they would come to know great joy—the greatest possible joy on earth. Despite the trials and tribulations of his life on earth, Jesus told them that he was a man of joy, and he prayed they would come to know and experience the same joy that filled him. He also predicted that he would soon be leaving them to prepare a place for them, not just after their death but here and now, on earth. It was a place where they could all again be one but in a different way.

The moment they lost sight of Jesus was the moment when he was reunited with his Father because his divine nature had been one with His Father from all eternity. However, now something new happened. The Son of God had returned home with a human nature that was, for the first time, united with God like never before. Now, in his human nature, he could contemplate the glory of God in such a way that God's glory utterly transformed him and the nature of his being. While being one with God in glory and in heaven, he would also be in the world in a new way. For now, in this new form of being, Christ could simultaneously be both in this world and in the next world. For he now had a Mystical Body that would expand to encompass the outer boundaries of the ever-expanding universe while at the same time drawing all who were open to receive him into his new glorified Mystical Body, where they would be one in him, and he would be in them.

3. Pentecost

If all was ready in heaven for what was to come next, all was not quite ready on earth. It would take time for the Apostles to process the events that took place at that first Easter, as they had all experienced untold physical and psychological pain and suffering. But they were also to experience the greatest joy that anyone could have. They needed time to reflect and pray and come to terms with the fear that was not unwarranted. They were still in Jerusalem, and they had been told to go out and preach the same message that Christ had preached. Would the same happen to them? The thought was unbearable, especially with the memory of Jesus' Passion still haunting them night and day.

Then, suddenly, things changed. Ten days later, their prayers were answered. Christ, as promised, returned with his Mystical Body, and the love that he received from his Father came pouring out. The outpouring of love was the Holy Spirit, his own personal fear-dispelling love. The new presence of Christ was even closer than before because before, they had been with him, but now, they were in him. Before, he could not be with even his closest disciples at all times. Now, he could and would be with all who would freely choose to receive him through the baptismal waters in a life consecrated to endlessly turning to receive the love he was always ready and able to give.

Who would not want to spend their lives repenting if it meant endlessly coming closer to Jesus and through him to the Father who had sent him? With their newly given love that casts out fear, they immediately went out to give the good news to a crowd of over three thousand, who, in their turn, also received the same Holy Spirit. The promised Holy Spirit had arrived, and the Church was founded. A new age began. It was the age of Christ the King and the Kingdom on earth exactly 'as it is in heaven'.

4. The Assumption.

Everyone present received the Holy Spirit in the Upper Room on that first Pentecost day, but one person received him more completely than any other. Because Our Lady was immaculately conceived, there was nothing in her that could prevent the Holy Spirit from totally possessing her and making so much possible for her and the newly founded Church. Now, her dear Son had not only risen from the dead, but he had returned, and he would never leave her again. Her total purity of heart and mind, yet to be achieved by the others, meant that the quality of her union with Jesus was as perfect as it could be for anyone on earth. Her cup was overflowing.

Peter may well be the Rock upon which the Church was founded, but Mary was now the very embodiment of her risen and Glorified Son, to whom all would turn as the Mother of the Church on earth. They would receive from her something of the love with which he now filled her. Her presence was, therefore, essential. Despite their closeness to Christ and the mutual love that bound them together while he was on earth, the Apostles were still spiritual adolescents. While, through daily repentance and prayer, they were becoming what the Holy Spirit would make of them, Mary would stand for them and others as the ideal to which they should all aspire. However, she did not stand there on a plinth to be duly admired and feted as Christ's mother; she had work to do that could not be done by another in quite the same way.

The apostles could see what Christ's love did for his mother, and they wanted that same love to do the same for them. At the very beginning, no one was more qualified than Our Lady, Mother of the Church, to teach them the only love that could enable them to love her Son as she did. That is why the new form of prayer that came to be called meditation owed more to her than to anyone else. For those who followed her teaching and still follow her teaching today, meditating on the most lovable man who ever existed on earth would gradually lead into the profound contemplative prayer that was her daily spiritual meat and drink. After purification, this new form of meditation would, like her own contemplation, lead them up and into Christ's own contemplation of his Father, even here on earth.

For this reason, God chose to leave Mary here on earth until at least the fledgling Church had sufficiently matured to manage without her earthly presence. Her assumption into heaven meant that her work was done, and God was calling her to her eternal reward.

5. The Coronation of Our Lady in Heaven

Once assumed into heaven, a coronation took place. It was the crowning of Mary as the Queen of Heaven and Mother of All who live and move in Christ in heaven and on earth. Now, the contemplation she enjoyed on earth—in, with, and through her Son—was brought to peak perfection. The absolute unfettered and unbridled love she experienced did not make her forget for a moment those whom she had left behind or those to whom she was called to be a mother in the future.

Her motherly wish for us is the absolute rapturous bliss which she enjoys now in heaven, contemplating her ever-loving Father together with her beloved, divine Son. This is why we have all been created in the first place, and this is why she was called to be the mother of her divine Son, who first showed us our infinite and blissful destiny and how to follow him there. The way, once clear, has now been blocked with the baggage of time and with the thankless, thoughtless and downright evil behaviour of those for whom Christ died such an agonising death.

The whole of human society, both inside and outside of the Church, has become so detached from the love with which Christ wanted us to be ruled that its opposite is now beginning to rule in its stead. Her appearance in recent years has one aim alone: to give us all another chance, even if it is in the last minute of extra time. Now is the time to listen to her and to follow her example. She makes it quite clear that if we do not, consequences will follow that are worthy of a loving God who has been rejected with all for which he stands.

CHAPTER 15

SELF-SACRIFICE AND THE SACRIFICE OF CHRIST

THE ROSARY DID NOT EXIST for hundreds of years, nor was it necessary for the early Christians who inherited a whole framework of daily prayers from their Jewish forefathers, which they adapted to their new religion. They would not only pray first thing in the morning and last thing at night but thrice daily in the synagogue and, on special feast days, in the Temple in Jerusalem. They would also pray before and after washing, before and after (and during) meals, before and after going out, and on innumerable other occasions.

When Our Lady appeared in recent years and asked people to pray, she could not possibly have introduced them to the whole daily framework of prayer that she was taught. As modern people have not only lost the knowledge of prayer but how to pray, she simply said, 'Pray the Rosary'. She knew that if they prayed the Rosary regularly and sincerely with humble hearts, she could and would lead them onwards to the heights of mystical union. The Rosary is Our Lady's choice of prayer because it is initially very easy, and everyone can begin using it immediately.

If we merely say the Rosary as best we can for a quarter of an hour or more each day, it is a great start. Why? Because we have freely started to give to God the most precious thing that we treasure: our time. When we turn to God in our prayer, we have repented, or turned to God. If we think it a waste of time because we have had a hundred and one distractions, then we are wrong because it means that one hundred and one times, we have turned back to God, or repented. In that time, we have practised what Our Lady asks of us—we have prayed and practised repentance. The sacrifice of our time and energy in doing this is then offered to God with our other sacrifices the next time we go to Mass. If we go to Mass with no offerings of our own to be united to the sacrifice of Christ, then we are no more than onlookers, not participators. So, when Christ comes physically within us, rather than being still to savour his sanctifying presence, we find it difficult to know what to say or do. Inevitably, we seek trivial reasons to evade prolonging what should be the most sublime moment in our lives.

The sacred Sunday liturgy, the supreme moment in our week, can become a rather irritating interruption to a day that most people deem 'sacred' because they wish it to be entirely devoted to their own good pleasure. This alone should show us just how far we have diverged from the days when our forebears suffered terrible and agonising deaths for the sake of the Holy Mass—a sacrament which even many believers treat with indifference, at least in practice. I am afraid that time is running out. Or at least it is running out for the ever-loving and ever-giving Father, who has had his infinite goodness thrown back in his face with ever-increasing insolence. Our Lady is warning us that enough is enough. God is not just love; he is also justice. And the time is upon us when his justice must be exercised.

Little time is left. We may lack sufficient time to become saints, yet we may have enough time to become penitents. God chastises the proud and the arrogant. Nevertheless, he cannot resist genuine sorrow, even from the worst sinners. Remember, it was to a former sex worker to whom he first appeared after the Resurrection, and it was to a convicted criminal to whom he offered forgiveness and promised instant entrance into heaven just before he died. It was a man who vociferously thrice denied him just before receiving his death sentence, whom he made the head of his Church. And it was a bloodthirsty Pharisee—a professional pursuant prosecuting the first Christians, throwing them into prison, flogging them and even sentencing them to death—whom he called to be the Apostle to the Gentiles. Nobody is beyond his mercy, even now at the eleventh hour. If it is indeed too late to become a saint, it is not too late to become a penitent. All that is needed is the humility to seek God's forgiveness that he always gives without delay. The pride that prevents us from beginning again is not the pride that precedes a fall but the pride that follows a fall. It is the pride that keeps putting off the forgiveness ever awaiting us when we seek it with a pure and humble heart.

If we choose to become penitents, then we must immediately begin to do what penitents do—and that is to repent. Prayer is where we begin to learn how to repent in set times for that purpose. For this reason, the mystic and mother, St Angela of Foligno, calls prayer the School of Divine Love. Because whatever form of prayer we use, we are continually turning our minds and hearts to God. St Francis said, 'It is in giving that we receive.' So, every time we raise our minds and hearts to give to God, he gives us the love that is our deepest desire. It is this grace that enables us to continue repenting as we turn in love to our husband or wife, father or mother, brother or sister, and then to the neighbour in need. When, therefore, we next go to Mass, the sacrifices that we have made in practising repentance are the offerings that unite us with the great sacrifice of Christ himself.

After we have praised, glorified, and adored Christ when we receive him in Holy Communion, it is the time to ask him to suffuse and surcharge our weak human love with his own divine love so that the quality of our repentance is deepened and strengthened with each passing week. In this way, our whole life gradually becomes the Mass, in which all we say and do is offered to God. In return, we receive the only love that can transform and transfigure us into the image and likeness of Jesus Christ, who can now reach out to others through us.

Chapter 16

From Meditation to Contemplation

LET US NOW LOOK in further detail at the Rosary to see how it can gradually lead to the heights of prayer for those who persevere. When we say the Rosary, repeating the Hail Mary fifty times, we are, in fact, asking Our Lady to pray for us and to help us. If we sincerely mean it and are not just using the Rosary as some sort of magical incantation, then Our Lady will listen to our pleas for help and do for us what can totally change our lives for good in this world and in the next. She can and will, as she always does, lead us to come to know and love her beloved Son more deeply. Therefore, we must meditate on the mysteries that will gradually enable us to deeply know and love her Son, Jesus, ever more personally. This can be difficult at first, as it was for me until the school's spiritual director gave me some advice.

He said Our Lady did not say that we should recite all the mysteries of the Rosary every day, nor did she insist that we say at least five decades each day. However, if we pray the Rosary, the same Holy Spirit who conceived Christ in her will teach us to meditate on God's love, embodied in her beloved Son, so he can be spiritually conceived in us. Because I found it difficult to recite the Hail Mary while meditating, he told me to pause at the end of each decade in order to meditate on the mystery to which it was dedicated. Consequently, if I said only one decade a day because the prayer became so absorbing and even led to contemplation, that would be fine. Never forget that the purpose of the Rosary is to lead us to come to know and love her Son.

After my meditation at the end of the decade, he taught me to say the Glory Be to thank God for his glorious plan of redeeming us. With the final 'Our Father,' we ask that he give us our daily bread, enabling us to play our part so that his Kingdom of Love and Peace in heaven be brought about on earth. Finally, when asking God to forgive us the sins preventing us from doing God's will, we ask God to do this according to the measure in which we forgive others' sins against us. If this becomes the way I say my daily Rosary, he insisted, then it would be ideal and enable the Holy Spirit to lead me on and into the contemplation that is Mary's prayer of choice.

When we come to love Christ more and more through meditation, he will grow in our hearts and minds and in our whole being. Love, in its very nature, wants to be united permanently with the one who is loved. This desire was made real for Our

Lady after the sending of the Holy Spirit on the first Pentecost day. She wants us to experience the same joy she experienced when she was intimately united with her Son in those early days of the Church. However, her mystical union with Christ, her Son, was so close, so intimate, and so ecstatically joyful because there was no sin in her that could possibly keep them apart for a single second. Whereas even though we have been baptised, we cannot have what she enjoyed until we have been sufficiently purified from the sinfulness preventing the loving union with Christ, which we yearn for with all our hearts.

After seven years as a Rosary Crusader, I entered the Franciscan novitiate as a teenager to try my vocation. Here, I spent two hours each evening after Compline, meditating particularly on the Passion and death of Christ. Eventually, it moved me to tears and led me to a spiritual climax in my

meditation, called Acquired Contemplation.
In this prayer, words give way to a silent,
loving gaze upon the One who gave his
all for us. This deeply emotional prayer
surcharged my already fever-pitch desire
for union with God. At this point in the
middle of my novitiate, everything that was
so sweet and pleasurable suddenly ended.
Without any warning, I was left in total
spiritual darkness, and there I remained for
over two years. I had not, like Mother Mary,
been immaculately conceived. So, the sin
and selfishness in me—the deep pride and
prejudice and all the other forces of evil that
lurked deep down in me that were never in
Our Lady—brought my prayer to an abrupt
end. It did this because it prevented the
profound mystical contemplation of God that
was and is, her daily prayer. I now thank God
for giving me the grace to persevere in this
dark and unintelligible world. I could not
have been given a greater grace. Whereas
before, while I was giving to God, I was

also receiving; whereas now, I had to learn to go on giving without receiving anything in return. In short, I had to learn perfect loving, which I had not been learning before. This alone would enable me to receive in greater abundance than ever before.

I have spent most of my life speaking and writing about this crucial period in the spiritual life when self-centred sinners are gradually transformed into God-centred believers who can begin to contemplate as Our Lady did and still does. Thus, for more details, you must explore my other works. Let me just say that in the darkest moment of my journey, I was led to the library to find and read the works of St John of the Cross and St Teresa of Avila. Without them, I would have been lost. Now, perhaps you can see why Our Lady has called herself 'Our Lady of Mount Carmel'; she is the patroness of the great Carmelite tradition, perfectly embodied in these two great Doctors of the

Church. Our Lady knows those who want to join her in her profound mystical prayer must first be purified of the sin and the residue of sin that was never in her. The best teaching is to be found in these two Carmelite mystics. Therefore, in all my own writings, I have tried to present their teaching in simple modern English.

Once we are purified, the Rosary, which had become all but impossible to pray as we would wish, becomes possible again to help us continue to meditate on the profound mysteries of our faith. Once we are sufficiently purified of the worst features of sin, the Holy Spirit can lead us into the profound mystical contemplation that is our Mother's prayer of choice. Like her contemplation, it will lead us on with her to enter into the mystical contemplation of Christ Our Lord. There, we will be able to gaze briefly, even in this world, on the glory of God. Furthermore, we will be able to receive from him the infused virtues and gifts of the Holy Spirit for others whom Christ has chosen to reach out to through us for his greater honour and glory and for the salvation of the world.

CHAPTER 17

A UNIQUE BIRTHDAY PRESENT

IF ST MARK'S GOSPEL can be called the Gospel of St Peter, then St John's Gospel can be called the Gospel of St Mary. Remember, she was the immaculate virgin whom God chose from eternity to become the human mother of his divine Son. She was also the virgin whom Christ himself, her own Son, had chosen while he was dying on the Cross to become the mother of St John. She lived with St John and mothered him for as many as twenty years after Christ bequeathed her to him. Before Pentecost, all the Apostles presumably lived in fear that what happened to Jesus would happen to them also. But after the sending of the Holy Spirit, they began to split up into separate homes, coming together for communal prayer and worship. It would have been, from then onwards, that St John would see his new mother like never before.

On the first Pentecost, Mary, together with the twelve Apostles, received the Holy Spirit. The first Apostles were still spiritual adolescents, as is evident to any objective reader of the scriptures. Yes, they received the Holy Spirit, but before he could possess them sufficiently to set the world on fire with the love of God, something had to be done first. For many years, they would have to practise for themselves the repentance they had told the crowds to practise in order to receive the Holy Spirit in sufficient fullness so as to bring Christ to life again in them. I do not believe in instant sanctity, nor were the Apostles an exception to the rule. Sanctity takes time—not months, but years. Original Sin twisted and contorted the Apostles like it does everyone else. It has distorted the nature that God gave all of us, made in his own image and likeness.

It did this in such a way that, as St Paul would explain in his letter to the Romans, it made him do the things he did not want to do while preventing him from doing what he genuinely wanted to do. Thus, on that first Pentecost day, the perfect Church would be seen only to the degree and to the extent that they all set out on the journey to find perfect love. On this journey, they would all support one another in practising the daily repentance that would enable them to become as perfect as possible in this vale of tears. For this reason, Christianity was initially called simply 'The Way'. However, on that unique birthday of the Church, God gave the first Christian followers a birthday present. It was not something but someone—a person who would not only be their human guide but show them their spiritual destination as embodied in a human nature like theirs. It was Mary who, for that very reason, came to be called not just the mother of John but the Mother of the

Church. Her Immaculate Conception meant that, although she received the Holy Spirit at the same moment as the Apostles, she was instantly united with her Son's risen and glorified body. This meant that their two Sacred Hearts were instantly united in love. So now, the Sacred Hearts of Jesus and Mary were simultaneously united in loving God the Father in an act of sublime mystical contemplation. What happened to her while she was still on earth would happen to those who would follow her example and her teaching, which she gave to all who sought it.

She taught firstly by example, as with her foster son, St John, she continued to practise the daily prayers they were taught as children. These prayers were gradually changed and reorientated to reflect that now and in future, they would be prayed in a new way. They would be prayed in, with, and through their Risen and Glorified Lord, in whose Mystical Body they now lived and moved and had their being. Once the framework for a life of daily prayer had been taught, Mary would be better placed than any other to introduce to others the new form of prayer, meditation. This would enable those who had never known Christ as she and the Apostles had to come to know and love him and the God who dwelt in him. When this love was ignited and burning with a deep desire to be united with him as she was, then her encouragement, teaching, and example would enable them to take the next step. It would enable the Holy Spirit to lead them into a new form of prayer called contemplation.

Mary's Immaculate Conception meant that she was immediately able to experience contemplation, as there was nothing to impede the action of the Holy Spirit, who would draw her up instantly. United with her beloved Son, she would experience something of the love of the One who dwells in Light Inaccessible. In contemplation, believers of 'The Way' would have to continue repenting by repeatedly turning to God, even though it seemed as if he had disappeared behind a 'Cloud of Unknowing'. If, despite the continual temptations to cut and run, believers would remain steadfast and persevere on 'The Way', encouragement would be given to keep offering themselves to God in the new worship in Spirit and in truth, carrying their daily cross.

In this way, true selfless loving would be learnt, and more quickly than before, so that the Holy Spirit could lead them into mystical contemplation, at least in some measure. St John of the Cross and St Teresa of Avila are the supreme doctors of the mystic way, where we are purified sometimes in the dark and sometimes in the light. That is why Our Lady calls herself 'Our Lady of Mount Carmel', for she is always there to encourage all who are prepared to carry their daily cross with Christ, in and outside of prayer, and so come to share in his glorious Resurrection.

Chapter 18

The Mystic Way

WHEN ST JOHN SAID that eternal life had already been given and could, therefore, be experienced in this life, he was not primarily speaking about his own experiences but what he saw being experienced by his new mother. Like any mother, she would have to make, mend, and wash her child's clothing, buy, prepare, and cook meals, and clean the home, making it cosy and welcoming, as well as all the many jobs mothers do. Nevertheless, when the day's work was over, she would find the space and time to turn to God to be replenished by her instant contemplation.

How many times would he have seen her experiencing Eternal Life as, together with her beloved Son, she prayerfully encountered the infinite glory of God enveloping, enthralling, and enrapturing her? Time and time again, he would have seen her utterly captivated by the ecstatic bliss that one day she would experience for all time when eternal life would totally consume every moment in heaven. When the Apostles practised what they preached for long enough, they too would come to know what it would be like to experience, at least some of the time, the eternal life and love that would ultimately possess them all of the time.

After ten years of what the historian Monsignor Philip Hughes called his 'novitiate', practising what he would soon be preaching to others, St Paul experienced something of the world to come, taking him completely out of himself. St Paul was, of course, speaking about himself and what he experienced at the end of his ten years of preparation for his task ahead as the Apostle to the Gentiles.

In his letter to the Corinthians, he put it this way: 'I will move on to the visions and the revelations that I have had from the Lord. I know a man who, fourteen years ago was caught up, whether in the body or out of the body, God knows, I do not know, right into the third heaven... into paradise and heard things which must not and cannot be put into human language' (2 Corinthians 12:1-5).

God does not just give the fruits of contemplation to pilgrims in moments of light, but in moments of darkness too that are far more common. We sometimes find that the journey is shrouded in darkness, and God seems to have turned his back on us. We begin to cry out as Christ did in his final moments on the Cross: 'My God, my God, why have you forsaken me?' Yet, when we faithfully travel on, regardless, then we are perhaps more open to receiving God's mystical or invisible love and the fruits of contemplation. As long as we continually try to journey onwards, to keep repenting, and to keep turning to God no matter what—even though we feel nothing—we will receive the fruits of contemplation. These fruits will gradually remake us in the image and likeness of the man in whose Name we have freely chosen to take up our daily cross. This is how God gives the infused virtues and the fruits of the Holy Spirit to pilgrims travelling the Mystic Way while remaining humble, as only the humble can speak to the proud and hope to be heard.

When Our Lady, St Paul, St John, and so many others tangibly experienced God's love in 'the contemplation of light', their humility always deepened. Encountering the magnificent power and the glory of God humbles us and makes us say with Our Lady, 'He who is mighty has done great things in me.' Witnessing the fruits of contemplation changing our and the lives of others, we know it is not our doing but God's doing, working through our human weakness. Profound contemplative prayer, encouraged and inspired by Our Lady, was practised by ordinary people in ordinary families long before religious life was even dreamt about. This is the prayer that had such a dramatic and ongoing effect in history. It changed a pagan empire into a Christian empire in an astoundingly short time. We know this for certain because, without the infused virtues and the supernatural gifts and fruits of the Holy Spirit, given only in such profusion in mystical contemplation, such a massive worldwide conversion could not possibly have occurred.

Nor will it ever be able to take place again at any future date without the Holy Spirit working through those who radically give their lives to him. Who could resist the quality of supernatural love quite evidently alive and thriving in the first Christians, which made them redolent with all the virtues their own religious and philosophical teachers lauded but never lived? All this was accompanied by the sort of humility unknown to a world that viewed humility as a weakness. Whereas, for Christians, it was the sole and indispensable foundation and basis for any successful spiritual life. Humility opens to receive the only love that can change the world. This is the quality of the humility that can alone be learnt on 'The Way'—the 'Mystic Way'—where we are purified at times in darkness and at times in light.

The most pernicious, perverting lie in the modern spiritual life is that contemplation is not for everyone but is rather an extraordinary and dangerous way for a few holy souls. Our Lady radically and clearly disagrees with such arrant nonsense. Only a new modern breed of radical contemplative Christians like those who were first inspired by Our Lady can do for the modern world what was done for the ancient world. It is time to go back to the future.

Mary's supreme example must have been crucial, as all the infused virtues and the gifts of the Holy Spirit were instantly embodied in her on that first Pentecost day. Now, she was indeed full of grace. If the newly baptised, as well as the Apostles, wanted to know where they were going and what would happen to them when they arrived, they could see this for themselves by looking at the mother of Jesus. He left her behind to be the Mother to the early Church as the perfect exemplification of what he wanted to see embodied in her new children.

Although St John did not actually write his Gospel until Mary returned to heaven, how could it not have been inspired and influenced by the Mother Jesus had given him moments before he died on the Cross? When Christ thought Mary had done what was necessary to be a Mother to the infant Church, he finally called her to heaven to become another mother. After her coronation as Queen of Heaven, her newfound life in the Mystical Body of her Son enabled her to become a mother once more. This time, it would not just be to those she left behind in space and time but to all future generations throughout the world. The mother Christ gave to St John moments before he died is now given to us all to the end of time. She is always ready and able to listen and to give her invaluable prayers for all who call upon her to help us in our need. The whole world needs her more now, perhaps more urgently than at any other time in history.

CHAPTER 19

MEDITATION AND THE MYSTERION

GOD'S INDESCRIBABLY MUNIFICENT and magnanimous plan, which St Paul described as the Mysterion—'God's secret plan'—is to share the infinite bliss he experiences in heaven with others. To do this, he created a three-dimensional world of space and time. It was created within his only begotten Son, who would be born into this world of an immaculate mother. Although he came into this world as its Lord and King, he did not come to lord it over anyone but to serve them. The service he came to perform for other human beings was to tell them of God's plan to share his infinite love with them and teach them how to receive it.

Let me now introduce you to a method of Rosary mediation which I have used for years that can enable you not just to meditate on God's plan as it can be seen unfolding while you say the Rosary but something further. This method can lead you into that plan as it is fully embodied in Jesus Christ. After making the Sign of the Cross, begin by saying a Hail Mary, but if you choose not to say nine more to honour the first of the joyful mysteries, let the first ten beads glide through your hands while you meditate on the Angel Gabriel appearing to Our Lady. The angel told her that from all eternity, in choosing to send his own Son to become a human being to proclaim and explain this plan, God simultaneously made her his immaculate mother. As the great theologian of the Immaculate Conception, Blessed John Duns Scotus, put it, 'If God chooses an end, he must choose the means.' Mary, daughter of Joachim, was that means, that human mother. To make this way of using the Rosary more powerful, reread all that the Gospels have to say about each mystery. This is essential, and hopefully, what

I have already written about them will be helpful, too.

When you have meditated on the Annunciation, for instance, without pausing, continue to the Visitation. Imagine yourself there, listening to what is being said, responding with your own words. Don't become merely an onlooker; become a participator, too. This mystery shows the absolute selfless humility of Our Lady. This is the very essence of her sanctity; despite recently hearing the world-shaking news, she thinks first of rushing to help an older cousin prepare to give birth rather than trumpeting her good news to the world. This cousin's child will be John the Baptist, the prophet who will announce Christ's coming and prepare people to repent so they may receive him. Little needs to be said of the birth of Christ himself, for the Christmas scene and its message is indelibly imprinted on our mind, our hearts, and our imaginations.

Our Lady wants us to say the Rosary and meditate on its mysteries to help us come to know and love her beloved Son. Therefore, when our meditation fills us with love, then we must pause to express our love in our own words. Consequently, we might meditate on no more than one mystery in the time available. All forms of prayer or devotion are to lead us on from what was before a predominantly nominal faith to a vibrant living faith. As our love for Christ begins to enthral us ever more deeply, it draws us into the love that bonds him to the Father. When the prayers of love generated in meditation lead us into contemplation, as they will do with perseverance, then they have achieved their objective. We are taken up with Mary, if only briefly, into the prayer she experiences.

I am simply introducing a different way of saying each decade of the Rosary that I and others have found helpful. When I was in the novitiate, it was while meditating on the sorrowful mysteries, slowly and prayerfully reading the profound mystical teaching that Christ gave to his Apostles at the Last Supper, that something dramatic happened. Only with hindsight did I realise I was led into mystical contemplation. It was not the contemplation of light but of darkness, because I had to be purified for two years before glimpses of light heralded a new beginning. It would be a new and more positive and enthralling form of contemplation for short periods of time. This form of contemplation enables us to experience for brief moments and in far less potency what Our Lady now experiences all the time.

We may well be rational animals, but to begin with, it is the animal instincts, impulses, and urges that predominate. Unless reason prevails in a form first imposed by our parents, teachers, and spiritual guides, then disaster will follow.

We will not go forwards but backwards. The spiritual life is rather like trying to run up a downward escalator. The moment you stop going forward, then you start going backwards. This backward movement can, unfortunately, begin at any time, or rather at the time when the rational influence of others ceases, and we freely choose to reject what was once imposed on us so we may go our own way. It does not take long to return to the self-satisfaction, pleasure, sensual indulgence, and self-seeking which becomes the main influence in our lives. Reason is then primarily used to rationalise our irrational behaviour to ourselves and to others.

What I have called 'dark contemplation' is the time when a sincere spiritual traveller is given the opportunity to act selflessly, to continually unite our sacrifices to the Sacrifice of Christ. That we seem to receive nothing in return only makes these sacrifices

more powerful before God, most particularly
when they are offered to him, in, with, and
through the supreme sacrifice of his Son,
Jesus Christ, at Mass and outside of Mass
in the privacy of our own hearts. Only the
relentless sacrificial offering of ourselves
in this way enables us to keep advancing
forward with the necessary purification,
leading to the endless ecstatic bliss God
has prepared for us. However, once we stop
moving forward and start moving backwards,
it is frightening to see that however high we
have risen, we can fall just as quickly. In no
time at all, we can find ourselves living by
instincts and desires we thought we had left
far behind.

When contemplative prayer is undermined,
if not ridiculed and therefore no longer
practised, then it is not only individuals
but whole sections of the Church that
risk slipping downwards toward perdition
while deceiving themselves into believing

otherwise. It is tragic to see so many backsliders today who seem to have radically fooled themselves. They seemingly believe they have been inspired to deem what up until was recently seen as right and wrong as now its opposite. And the clear teaching of Jesus Christ is sadly seen as but an outdated teaching of a man who, had he lived today, would agree with their perversion of God's sacred and irreversible teaching.

Now, we can see why Our Lady calls herself 'Our Lady of Mount Carmel', for it is most particularly in the mystic way that she wishes to help us. It is here that she supports us more than at any other time while we try to develop from spiritual adolescents into spiritually mature adults. It is here, when darkness seems to reign supreme and even God seems to have forgotten us, that our love is finally purified as we cooperate with the Holy Spirit, whose love inspires and strengthens us. Now, a person is sufficiently purified and able to experience true contemplation with Our Lady, receiving as she did the fruits of contemplation. This is the way we can do for the modern world what Our Lady and the first Christians did for the ancient world.

When you naturally finish meditating on each mystery, simply move on to the next, allowing the ten beads to glide through your hands, pausing to complete your meditation before turning your attention to the next mystery. If the whole time for prayer involves meditating on only one or two mysteries, then that is fine and even better if it leads into contemplation, as it inevitably will in God's good time, not yours. End your prayer time with another Hail Mary, then a Glory Be, and finally with the Our Father, followed by the Sign of the Cross.

Chapter 20

Contemplation and the Mysterion

AFTER THE TERRIBLE EVENTS of the first Good Friday, Our Lady must have been traumatised like never before, and her pure and sensitive nature must have multiplied the sufferings that no other mother would have to endure before or since. There was no doubt that this suffering would have been alleviated by the Resurrection of her beloved Son, but what was done to him would still haunt her night and day. The mystery of what happened to him, and why, would take some time for her to appreciate.

In the days between his Resurrection and Pentecost, she would continue to pray according to the pattern of daily prayer to which she was accustomed. She would have hours to reflect and meditate on the past, beginning with that epoch-making moment when she was told she was to become the Mother of God. However, when on the first Pentecost day she received the Holy Spirit, something happened that had never happened in quite the same way. She was spiritually and mystically lifted up and into her divine Son, though her body still remained on earth. From now on, as mother to St John and as Mother to the Church, her prayer would have a totally new and dramatic supernatural dimension. If she began to meditate on the terrible past that ended on Calvary, she would be lifted out of herself into her beloved Son. Here, she would be enveloped by her love for him and his love for her. Together, they would gaze upon the infinite glory of the Three-in-One, in whom we are all called to dwell as to our final destiny, when God's plan, his Mysterion, would be brought to completion.

In this new contemplative loving, she would leave all her sorrows on earth behind her, at least for a time, as the love of the Father who first conceived her possessed her physical and spiritual motherhood. In these moments of ecstatic fulfilment, her motherhood would be continually suffused and surcharged by divine love to enable her to be the mother Christ had given to St John and to the infant Church, until having her work done, she would be crowned in heaven. Here, she would experience for all time what on earth she had, like those who would follow her example, experienced for only some of the time.

To understand her unique and indispensable role in the early Church, the quality of Our Lady as the most perfect woman and mother who ever lived must be fully appreciated. When God conceives a plan, he provides the means for its perfect implementation. If his only begotten Son was to have a human mother, then he would make sure that she was perfect in every way for the purpose for which he would create her. Her human mind and heart would be faultless, flawless, and forever expanding to enable her to play her remarkable part in God's Plan, the Mysterion.

To this end, her Immaculate Conception would enable God's love to penetrate, permeate, and pervade all her human faculties so she could fill the role he had prepared for her to perfection. On the first Pentecost day, her new supernatural oneness with her beloved Son would enable him to remain with his first disciples, most especially through her. Who was able to understand and practise her Son's sublime mystical teaching better than everyone else, with the human gifts he had brought to perfection in her? She was not left behind to be the Queen of Heaven in waiting, to receive the homage, the veneration, and the obeisance of her new subjects. Like her Son, her royal status was not given to be served by others but to serve them as she did. She was a practical working mother, not just to St John, but to the infant Church who would have turned to her as the fons et origo, the fountain, not just of all the divine wisdom that permeated the teaching of her Son but of how to put that wisdom into practice through prayer and good works.

Has there ever been a more qualified and perfect spiritual director than Mary, our mother? She wishes to continue to do for us now what she did for others in the infant Church. She wants to teach us how? Through meditation. Through reflecting on and praying about what Jesus did for us in the past. The same Holy Spirit who led her onwards can lead us onward into contemplation. Perfect contemplation means joining her to contemplate the glory of God, in and together with her Son, now risen and glorified. Whilst she was able to do this instantly and to perfection on the first Pentecost day and on every subsequent day, something has to happen to us before we can follow where she desperately wants to lead us. We are not immaculately conceived like her; therefore, the sin, selfishness, pride, prejudice and self-seeking all must be purified. It must be sufficiently purified so that our imperfect contemplation can become perfect contemplation even in this life. She has shown us the way and begs us to follow her.

When she speaks to little children to call the rest of us back to the practice of our faith as it was practised under her guidance in the early Church, she can only, of necessity, speak in the simplest of terms so that all can understand. She calls us all, therefore, to repent, to turn back to God, to begin again, and to keep making sacrifices. These acts of self-giving are formed more effectively through prayer than anywhere else, where we continually try to raise our hearts and minds to God for that purpose. These acts of selflessness enable God's love to bring our love to ever greater perfection. Gradually, those who persevere will generate, under the inspiration of the Holy Spirit, a supernatural habit of loving for our own salvation and the salvation of others who see God at work in us. The sacrifice learnt in opening ourselves to the love of God should then, Our Lady insists, be offered with the whole Christian Community at Mass, which took place every Sunday in the early Church. Here, what is given is returned by God a hundredfold.

In this way, we are continually caught up in a daily liturgy of giving and receiving to God and for others as Christ is being formed in us. The key moment in anyone's spiritual life is when, after meditation, we are led into contemplation. It is here that we are prepared to share in the contemplation of Christ himself, as Mary, our mother, did on earth and does now continually in heaven. As it is impossible for Our Lady to explain and detail clearly what is happening at this crucial moment in the spiritual life and how to press on to join her in perfect contemplation, she does something else. She reveals herself as Our Lady of Mount Carmel so that we can turn in our need to St John of the Cross and St Teresa of Avila, for even she cannot condense over six large volumes of their profound teaching in such a short time and to such unlearned children.

It has been my life's work trying to make the remarkable teaching on contemplation of these Doctors of the Church accessible to all. Still, please remember that some of the greatest saints could hardly read or write, yet they did have a mother to turn to, as do we. She will never fail and ever support those who are prepared to follow her simple teaching on prayer every day of their lives. And despite all the darkness, all the dryness and aridity, all the temptations and distractions that assail us, she will lead us on to join her to come to know and experience the love that surpasses all understanding. She will help us share this love with a world that is lost without it. She will do this without fail for all who call upon her for help because she is Our Lady, Our Lady of Mount Carmel.

Chapter 21

Miracles, Signs and the Mysterion

I HAVE NEVER MET a scripture scholar who appreciates the debt St John owed to Our Lady for the Gospel he wrote, nor how deeply she influenced him and his sublime masterwork. When St John took her into his own home to look after her physically, she looked after him spiritually. St John was still the same callow youth who had only recently asked Christ to call down thunder from heaven to destroy a town that rejected him. He wanted to be given a place of high honour in his Kingdom, and yet he ran away with the others when Christ was arrested. He had much to learn, and what he learnt was from the most gifted, the wisest, and the holiest person on earth.

Is it the fear of being influenced by pious speculation that makes scholars looking for clear and coherent evidence, discount her enormous influence on his most profound Gospel? The truth of the matter is that the woman God chose as the mother of his Son, Jesus, was chosen by Jesus himself to be a mother to his beloved disciple, John. Was not Christ himself aware of the influence that his mother, who had such an influence on his own upbringing, would have on his favourite disciple's spiritual development? And, through him, on the future spiritual development of his Church? Why else did Jesus bequeath his mother to St John and she to him with his dying breath on his hideous deathbed. They did not spend their time discussing the weather or the price of food. Her beloved Son would have been the centre of their conversation. How to further God's plan, preached and practised by Jesus before he taught it to others, would have been their daily talking point. They would reflect together on the deeper inner meaning of all that Jesus said before and after his public ministry began. What the other disciples only learnt gradually, St John learnt before everyone else because he had the best Christian teacher the world has ever known, living with him in his own home, teaching him day after day.

What would have been immediately obvious to him when they set up their home together would be something that happened instantly to Our Lady on the first Pentecost day. But it would be something that no one noticed at the time. This was because the sending of the Holy Spirit had such a dramatic effect on the Apostles and on the three thousand or more who listened to St Peter's sermon that all attention was elsewhere. What St John would have realised with hindsight after seeing his foster mother daily lost in ecstatic contemplation was that this happened to her on that first Pentecost day. It happened instantly upon receiving the Holy Spirit because her Immaculate Conception meant that there was no stain of sin whatsoever in her, which could impede the action of God's love. It was this Love, the Holy Spirit, that immediately possessed her. It instantly drew her up and into her beloved Son, now risen and glorified in heaven, and, together with him, she would be enwrapped in the contemplation of their heavenly Father.

In this sublime prayer, she would receive, in ever-increasing fullness, the eternal life or the transforming love of God that would make her the mother of all the virtues and all the gifts and fruits of the Holy Spirit. Just as the risen and glorified Christ was central to Mary's daily prayer and spirituality, St John made the Risen Christ—or as some scripture scholars have called him, 'Christ the Eternal Contemporary'—central to his Gospel. Learning from his foster mother, the Risen Christ became the supreme and ever-continuing sacrament of God's Love, alive and loving in the Church, founded in his name. All the other sacraments to which he referred are given to incorporate us into Our Risen Lord, and everything else he said and did were to help continue to support and strengthen his future disciples as they travelled along 'The Way' in, with, and through Christ towards their eternal destiny.

This was most particularly true of the Sacrifice of the Mass, where Mary would offer everything, in, with, and through her Son to the Father—all that she had said and done the previous week. Then, in return, her precious Son entered into her to suffuse and surcharge her love with his own when she received him physically within her as the 'Bread of Life', about which, as might be expected, St John wrote so profoundly in the sixth chapter of his awe-inspiring Gospel. It was Our Lady who taught him to see all this, taught him to see and understand what the other Gospel writers did not see with the same clarity and depth, at least at the time they wrote their Gospels. Take the miracles as a case in point. They were a clear indication that the power of God was at work in Jesus and, therefore, proof of who he was and claimed to be, but they meant something else too. These miracles were an outward sign of the loving-kindness of God made present, made visible in the most perfect, loving, and adorable man who ever lived.

Still, they signified something further. That is why, unlike the other Gospel writers, St John called Christ's miraculous actions 'signs', and so does Jesus himself (John 6:26). They were the signs that the one who performed them wanted those who received them to see their deep and everlasting significance. They were the signs that the Risen Lord, who was now alive and loving them, was always present to raise them both physically and, more importantly, spiritually. Christ's miracles are the clear signs that he would always be with us to bring the dead back to life again—not just those who were physically dead, but those spiritually dead too. He would always be with us, not just to bring back to full health those with physical sickness but also those with spiritual sickness. He would always be there, not just to cure external maladies but internal maladies of mind and heart. And not just to restore physical sight and hearing but the life-changing spiritual sight and hearing as well.

All too often, the miracles that have accompanied Our Lady's appearances over the last hundred and fifty years or more have been seen only on the physical level as signs of the presence of God's power working through her and of her loving care and kindness for all who pray to her. These are the signs and wonders that are the usual topic of conversation when pilgrims return home from Marian Shrines, and they are the spiritual memories that keep them going in the day-to-day practice of their faith in the future. This is fine and good, but, like St John, we must learn to see another, deeper dimension to these miracles or signs that Our Lady would have taught St John to see and understand. They were meant to affect people, not just with the experience of wondrous events to be shared with their family and friends, but to inspire them to live ever deeper spiritual lives. They were meant to raise them from the death of their previous superficial lives. They were meant to bring us back to full spiritual health and then to see, hear, and experience something of what St John calls 'Eternal Life', even here and now in this life, as Mary herself experienced it.

That which she experienced, she calls us onward to experience, too. This love contains all the infused virtues and the gifts of the Holy Spirit, which will enable us to say with

St Paul, 'I live, no, it is not I who live, but Christ who lives in me' (Galatians 2:20). This can be experienced here and now in this life, as St John saw for himself when he saw his mother regularly taken out of herself in prayer, enwrapped in the love that is beyond understanding. Do I need to spell out the sacrifices she asks us to make in our day so we may come to know and experience the Love she experienced in her day? This will enable all who follow her example to receive the fruits of this Eternal Loving that can transform and transfigure us as it transformed and transfigured Our Lady. St John did not see this happen only to Our Lady but also to those others whom Mary, our Mother, taught, namely the first generation of the Catholic Church.

CHAPTER 22

THE ROSARY AND THE MYSTERION

BEREFT OF THE SOLID FOUNDATION of a daily prayer life that was commonplace to her first children, Our Lady is today teaching a new way of following her prayerful way to God. It is, as we all well know, called the Rosary. It begins on one spiritual level, but it gradually leads all with ears to hear with, eyes to see with, and hearts to love with, on to an ever-deeper level until our prayer life corresponds to her contemplative prayer life. At first, we say the Hail Mary over and over again, and for a time, this is excellent. However, it should finally dawn on a person that the Hail Mary is essentially a prayer of petition, asking Our Lady to pray for us. If we who recite the Rosary are sufficiently sincere, humble, and open to Our Lady's response to our petitions, she will lead us onwards to her Son, to come to know and love him as she does. In other words, for those who find it difficult to say prayers and meditate at the same time, we can give less time to the saying of prayers and more time to meditating on each mystery of God's Plan. In this way, we will be doing what Our Lady wants us to do more than anything else, namely, to come to know and love her beloved Son ever more deeply.

When our love for him reaches its limit, Our Lady knows better than anyone that our love, tainted with self-love, must be purified so we may love Christ as she does in the pure and simple contemplation that she enjoys at all times. United with her, and in, with, and through her beloved Son, we are guided through every stage of our spiritual life to our final destiny in heaven.

Do not think that pilgrimages to Marian Shrines are ends in themselves.

They are not just for spiritual 'top ups' to help us carry on as before, skimming along the surface of our Catholic faith, albeit reinvigorated. Our Lady appeared to inspire us to do much, much more. She is calling us to follow her by showing us how to generate the powerful sublime love that can be given us only by the Holy Spirit as we come to know and love God ever more deeply. Once our self-centred and self-seeking love has been purified, this love will lead us into the profound mystical contemplation Mary shares with her Son. Here, we are all united as one as we journey onward toward our final destiny into what is called Light Inaccessible.

If pilgrims to Marian Shrines did this over the last hundred and fifty years, and so, therefore, did what the first Christians did for the ancient pagan world, then Our Lady would not have had to come to warn us that God is poised to punish the world. It did not seem to go deeper, leading us on, radically and unconditionally, to consecrate our lives to our Risen Lord like our first Christian forebears, come loss of all possessions, come humiliation, come imprisonment, come torture and death. It has been estimated that far more people have been to Marian Shrines in the last hundred years, as there were Christians in the first century after the Resurrection. Why have they not had the same impact on today's pagan world as the first Christians did on the ancient pagan world? The difference is that we think that we can have it both ways. We think that we can continue to enjoy the material pleasures of the pagan world in which we live while continuing to enjoy the spiritual benefits of our Catholic faith. Our first Christian forebears knew they could not. But after three centuries, when they began to think and act as if they could enjoy the best of both worlds, as we do today, the decline, deterioration, and decadence of our faith set in, from which we have never fully recovered.

Like Our Lady, St Paul knew what it was like to be taken out of himself in pure otherworldly contemplation. However, because he then received the fruits of contemplation, he not only lived but preached the whole of the Gospel, loud and clear, and so suffered the consequences. Because he refused to compromise with the world, he was scourged like his Master five times, stoned and beaten with sticks, and finally brutally put to death for the faith that we all too easily take for granted. Have we been genuinely and deeply inspired by Our Lady's apparitions? If so, then we should newly and continually reconsecrate our lives to following her teaching and example. Such dedication will compel us to forgo compromise with a world poised to persecute us for refuting the monstrous moral malaise into which it has fallen. Remember the words of Christ, 'To those who much has been given, much will be expected' (Luke 12:48). We must learn to see and understand what Our Lady taught St John. Miracles are signs, too, and they are even more important for what they signify because they lead us, at least for those who can see, into the One who originally performed them.

CHAPTER 23

THE SIN AGAINST THE HOLY SPIRIT

AS WE HAVE SEEN, Our Lady's Immaculate Conception meant that there was no sin in her. This meant that there was no impediment within her to prevent the continual and ongoing inflow of the Holy Spirit, who immediately filled her on the first Pentecost day and drew her up and into her loving Son. Here, she shared and enjoyed with him the sublime contemplation of God the Father, where together they contemplated his Glory. Seeing what happened to the Mother Jesus had given them, the first Christians saw what would happen to them also once they were purified by daily practising the repentance first learnt in the school for divine loving, which is prayer.

Long before St Paul said, 'I live, no it is no longer I who live, but Christ who lives in me' (Galatians 2:20), Our Lady could say these words the moment she received the Holy Spirit with the Apostles in the Upper Room. Seeing her and what she did each day, and how she did it, they were looking at what the Holy Spirit would do for them if they kept repenting. In those early days, there was only one outstanding and unforgivable sin, and that was the sin of omission, which Our Lady has said in modern times is the worst of all sins. It is what Jesus himself called 'the sin against the Holy Spirit' and is committed today more than any other sin. It is the father and the mother of all the sins for the faithful, as despite all God has done, and all his Son has suffered to ensure that the Holy Spirit would be poured out on the first Pentecost day and on every subsequent day, we fail and continually fail to keep turning to receive it.

Disaster will follow because we commit the sin against the Holy Spirit for which, as Christ himself insisted, there is no forgiveness. This point is of such importance that it needs further explanation. In recent years, Our Lady has made it quite clear that the sin of omission, which prevents the Holy Spirit from entering our lives to change them, is the most pernicious sin of all. At the Last Judgement, we will see our sins, not as others see them, or even as we think we see them ourselves, but as God sees them. When this happens, we will see that the greatest sin of all has been the sin of omission, or the sin against the Holy Spirit. Theologians do not consider it good theology to project human feelings into God. However, this did not deter the greatest theologian of all. When only one of the ten lepers he cured came to thank him for curing them, he was deeply hurt. Furthermore, he frequently explained how his Father is deeply insulted when his many invitations, gifts, and blessings to his people have been received with indifference or disdain, if not outright contempt. Nor did he refrain from describing what God would do to those who did this. Jesus made it quite clear that if God's love and the Holy Spirit who transmits that love to us is continually treated with contempt, frightening consequences will follow.

Jesus called this indifference, this disdain or contempt, the sin against the Holy Spirit for which there is no forgiveness. Forgiveness, like all the other gifts of God, comes through his love, as it is being received into an open and willing human heart. If you close your mind and heart to God and his love and stop daily repenting, you close it to all else he wants to give you, which comes only through his divine love. This, of course, includes the forgiveness we all need and crave. The longer we sin against the Holy Spirit by refusing to open ourselves to his love, the quicker we go backwards on that spiritual escalator that relentlessly draws us downward—further away from God and the only love that can save us from disaster. To guarantee this will never happen to us, we must follow the example of our first Christian forebears by continually repenting, by continually turning lovingly to God daily to receive his love that is at all times poised to possess us, or else we will be led into 'The Sin against the Holy Spirit'.

Our Lady, the Apostles, and the first followers of Jesus continued to turn and open themselves to receive God's love, his Holy Spirit, through daily and ongoing prayers. These prayers were the daily prayers they were taught as children; however, they gradually changed them to introduce new prayers reflecting that thenceforth, they would be directing their prayer to their same Father as before, but in, with, and through Jesus Christ, their Risen Lord and Saviour. This would not only infinitely multiply the power of their prayer to God but multiply what he could give them in return. If they wanted to know where this prayer was leading them, they needed only to look at the Mother Jesus gave while on the Cross to St John and to the infant Church.

St John of the Cross gives us an extremely helpful example to explain the inner nature of the repentance learnt in prayer. When Moses and all the families watched with ever-increasing horror as their young men were being cut down in the terrible carnage during the battle against the Amalekites, they all but despaired. Despite the temptation to gaze upon the awful bloodshed of his beloved people, which he could do nothing to prevent, Moses kept trying to turn to the only One he knew could help him. Time and time again, he repented, turning to God by raising his arms aloft in prayer and begging for his intervention. But, time and time again, as if by some malign magnetic force, he was drawn back to witness the evil that was being perpetrated on the battlefield before him. Seeing how God was beginning to act through him to bring about victory when he prayed, his bodyguards propped up his arms, keeping them raised to God in prayer. Victory came quicker than expected, lives were saved, evil was prevented, and peace prevailed.

The same happens when we drag ourselves away from the evils of the world, which are daily set before us through the all-enveloping power of the mass media. When, like Moses, we turn to the only One who can prevent it and turn time and time again to him as we wrestle with the pernicious powers of evil, we are practising repentance in our daily prayer. This is the inner repentance, practised in our minds and hearts, that repeatedly opens us to the only love that can change us. Only this love can bring us to the peace for which we yearn, making us into channels of peace for others. The props used to help Moses keep his heart and mind fixed on God symbolise the spiritual props or prayers that we use to help us keep repenting and keep turning our hearts and minds to God until they remain sufficiently open to receive his love and all the infused gifts contained within that love. The selflessness practised and the love received in this prayerful action can alone facilitate the selflessness practised outside of prayer, as we keep trying to love God in the neighbour in need, beginning with our own families.

Then, the sacrifices made whilst practising repentance could be offered at Mass to be united with the Sacrifice of Christ and receive in return the hundredfold that Jesus promised. The whole of the spiritual life can be summed up in the four words used by Our Lady: Repent, Pray, Sacrifice, and the Mass. When this spiritual dynamic of what has been called 'sacrificial repentance' is practised day after day, week after week, year after year, we are taken into and fitted ever more fully into Christ's sacrificial action that we celebrate every time we go to Mass. Regardless of what we believe in our minds, if this daily 'sacrificial repentance' is not practised with our hearts, then we will soon be committing the 'sin against the Holy Spirit' and will inevitably be travelling downward on the ladder of perfection, or what I have called the spiritual escalator. We reside in the last minute of extra time. Start again—beginning now—to turn again daily to the only One who can change you and the world that Christ has chosen to redeem through you.

Although in this book I am not writing a work of detailed scholarship, all that I am saying is based on many decades of studying the profound God-given spirituality which Jesus introduced into the early Church. This is the same spirituality that was first seen and practised to perfection by his own mother. I am not, therefore, going to show step-by-step and in detail how the Jewish pattern of prayer that Jesus inherited was transformed, thanks to him and his mother and the first disciples, into early Christian prayer. Rather, what follows is a blueprint for daily prayer based on and inspired by the prayer life of our first Christian ancestors. This blueprint is based on years of biblical and extra-biblical study. It is a summary of what I have detailed in my book, Wisdom from the Christian Mystics.

CHAPTER 24

MORNING PRAYER

THIS BLUEPRINT FOR DAILY PRAYER is a
modern Christian reconstruction of the prayer
Our Lady was taught by her parents and
which she taught her Son, Jesus. After the
sending of the Holy Spirit, she, together with
all the Apostles and new disciples, realised
that spiritual life would be significantly
different. Henceforth, they would proceed
as St Luke described; they would 'live and
move and have their very being' in their Risen
Lord in his new and glorified Mystical Body.
Here, they would pray at all times with and
through him. As he taught them, their new
and ever-loving Divine Dad would be the
object of their prayer, and that is why the
very prayer he gave them, the Our Father,
was the most commonly used communal and
personal prayer.

Therefore, to introduce you to the new daily prayer life that Our Lady would have used together with his other disciples, I will use each letter of the Our Father for the blueprint to help you to learn how to pray each day, as she did in her day, albeit with several accommodations. These reminders may be accommodated to the modern world by using modern examples and the inspirations of the saints who have followed in her footsteps over the centuries.

The first three letters of the Our Father, O-U-R, in the blueprint will remind us of the three essential features of morning prayer. The letter O would remind us to say the morning Offering in one form or another. The letter U would remind us that as we make this prayer, like Mary herself, we are Uniting ourselves with Christ, her Son, and with all who are in him. Then, the letter R would remind us to make Resolutions for the coming day, resolving to do all and everything for the honour and glory of God. Then, every letter of the word Father could be used, too, to remind us how to pray during the day or night at a time set aside for that purpose.

The letter F will be a reminder to make an act of Faith, enabling us to express our belief as simply as possible and in our own words, in the God who is an ever-loving Father, in Jesus, his ever-loved and ever-loving Son, and in the Holy Spirit, who draws us all back through Jesus into God's Kingdom of Endless Loving. Once we have briefly meditated on what God has done for us and is continuing to do for us, it is time to make our response. To do this, the remaining letters of the word Father can be used accordingly. The letter A stands for Abandonment, T' or Thanksgiving, H for Holy Communion, E for Examination of conscience, and, finally, R for Repentance. To

242

help beginners, I have included nine prayers that, with use, we can transpose into our own words to make them more personal.

Thus, the acronym looks like so:

O   Offering

U   Uniting

R   Resolutions

F   Faith

A   Abandonment

T   Thanksgiving

H   Holy Communion

E   Examination of conscience

R   Repentance

1. The Morning Offering

The first word, OUR, can help remind us how
to make our morning prayer. The letter O
can remind us to make our Morning Offering.
For Our Lady, this morning offering took
the form of what was called the Shema, in
which she promised to commit herself to
loving God with her whole mind and heart,
with her whole body and soul, and with
her whole strength. We can do the same
in our own way and in our own words,
as Mary did the moment she woke in the
morning. My mother taught me to make my
morning offering to dedicate the whole of
the forthcoming day to God, to show that
I loved him with my whole being as Mary
did, and to promise to try and show my love
for him in the forthcoming day. My mother
told me that by offering all I said and did
to God in the day ahead of me, I could
become, as she put it, 'a little priest turning
ordinary commonplace things into something

precious, as Rumpelstiltskin turned straw into gold'. When our family went to Mass each Sunday, they saw their mother totally absorbed in what they all too easily took for granted. Their selfishness meant they had too little to offer, while she was offering a thousand and one acts of self-sacrifice made for them during the previous week. Each day, she reminded herself of this, her sacred calling, by making her Morning Offering as her recusant ancestors did for hundreds of years before her.

When Pope Benedict XVI was approached by a young couple who had five children and an extremely busy schedule every day to feed, clothe, and educate them, they asked him a question. It was a question they had been asking themselves but to which they could find no answer. 'How can we possibly find time for prayer?' they asked. 'Our days are so full.' They never forgot the Holy Father's answer. 'By beginning each day with the

Morning Offering,' he said, 'so that your whole life can become a prayer, just as the whole life of Jesus was a prayer because he offered up everything he said and did to his Father in heaven.'

If ever I forgot to say mine, my mother would remind me that St Jean-Baptiste Vianney, the Curé d'Ars, would say, 'All that we do without offering it to God is wasted,' and he was right.

Let us always ensure that we begin each day with a morning offering:

God, our Father, I wish to consecrate all that I say and all that I do to you in this forthcoming day, just as Jesus did every day of his life on earth. Please accept what I do so imperfectly and unite it with the perfect offering that Jesus continues to make to you in heaven. I offer to you my joys and my sorrows, my successes as well as my failures, because these especially show how much I have need of you. I make my prayer in, with and through Jesus, in whom we all live and move and have our being. Amen.

2. Union with Christ

Now for the letter U. It was my mother who first taught me something that Our Lady herself came to realise after her Son's glorification. She said that even though I may make my morning offering alone by the side of my bed, I am not alone. My prayer is always made in, with, and through Jesus, and so with all other Christians, wherever they are. The great Jesuit liturgist Father Joseph Jungmann said, 'Christ does not offer alone, his people are joined to him and offer with him and through him. Indeed, they are absorbed into him and form one body with him by the Holy Spirit who lives in all.'

This also means we can pray to and with all the saints who are alive in Christ as we are and with and for all our own relatives and friends, too, both living and dead, who are alive in him. She especially taught me to pray in the same way for the Holy Souls in purgatory. My mother also told me that this was the perfect opportunity to pray for others, too, especially those who have asked me to pray for them. She said that when you hear about people who are suffering all over the world, on the radio, on television, or in the newspaper, you can reach out to them through prayer because prayer is not limited by space and time as we are. The wonderful thing about praying for others in the morning is that they can be included in the prayer that becomes the rest of our day.

St Padre Pio was praying when a lay brother, believing that he was out, burst into his room to find him lost in prayer. The saint dismissed his apologies with the words, 'I was just praying for a happy death for my father.'

'But your father died two years ago!' the brother said, looking rather surprised. Padre Pio looked at him in disbelief and said, 'I know he did.'

True Christian prayer is not limited to the world of space and time in which we live; it takes us into another dimension where, in the Mystical Body of Christ, it can reach out now to help those in need, to the four corners of the world, and just as easily to the needy in the past and in the future. That is why the Church made St Thérèse of Lisieux, a young, enclosed Carmelite nun, the patroness of the missions.

Speaking on the radio, a Catholic doctor who was tortured in a Chilean jail said that she received tremendous help from the prayers of friends back home. She likened their prayers to 'waves of love' that sustained her through some of the darkest moments of her ordeal. On the same news program, I heard the story of a group of Christians suffering in Chinese indoctrination camps who risked their lives to smuggle a tape recording out to their brethren in the West begging for their prayers. Suffering makes people of deep faith sensitive to the extraordinary power of prayer.

We may unite ourselves to God with a prayer such as the following:

Father, I know that the more your Holy Spirit draws me into your Son, Jesus, the more I am united to all who are within him. I, therefore, ask Mary and Joseph, Peter and Paul, and all the saints, especially those to whom I have a special devotion, to be with me now as I pray so that my prayers may be fortified by theirs. I also want to pray for my family and friends and all who have asked me to pray for them. May they benefit from the day ahead that I wish to become a perfect prayer as I offer all I say and do to you through Jesus Christ, Our Lord. Amen.

3. Resolutions for the Day Ahead

The third letter in my blueprint is R to remind us that, despite what I have just said, the Morning Offering is not a magic formula. It does not automatically transform the forthcoming day; therefore, something further is required. Spend a few minutes reviewing the day ahead, making a few resolutions which would enable you to consecrate every moment of the day to loving God.

Such a resolution may be to pause for brief moments of prayer during the day, as Our Lady and the early Christians did, but also in sacrificing to do humdrum tasks that we keep postponing, such as changing the bedsheets, putting air into the car tyres, defrosting the freezer, or something more pressing. Alternately, we may attend to a friend or relative who is sick or in need; write a letter, ring the telephone, send a quick text, or even visit for a few minutes. We may have to make a resolution to apologize to a family member, a friend, or a coworker for our previous poor behaviour. Admittedly, it is very difficult to stand up for someone who has been abused by an authority at work or elsewhere, to speak the truth when no one wants to hear it or to make a stand for what we know is right. Nevertheless, these are some significant endeavours we might include as part of Morning Prayer.

Pause briefly to make resolutions for the day ahead:

Jesus, help me to review the day ahead to anticipate all that I should do so that I can resolve to love God as you did, through everything I do and love my neighbour too, as you love all of us. Help me to forgive my enemies as you forgave, as well as my friends. And give me the grace to seek forgiveness from those I have offended and never to cease trying to be like you and to behave like you in all that I say and do. Amen.

Chapter 25

Daily Prayer

ST ANGELA OF FOLIGNO, a mother like Mary, said that prayer is the School of Divine Love, where we learn how to love God. It is here that our efforts at loving God enable him to love us in return. Love cannot be forced on anyone against their will. This is true of both human and divine love, so unless we try to love God as best we can, his love cannot be forced. Forced love is simply a contradiction in terms.

Prayer is the practice we employ to keep trying to love God, knowing that God cannot resist loving those who seriously and genuinely desire to love him. Our sincerity is proved firstly through how we make daily time to love him in prayer and secondly, through continually trying to express our love for him during that time.

Let me now turn to evening or night prayer, beginning with an Act of Faith.

4. An Act of Faith

The letter F can remind us to start by making an Act of Faith. I do not mean by reciting some traditional formula of faith or even professing belief in every article of the creed or in every dogma the Church teaches. There is a time and place for that, but this is the time for something else. Our faith is not firstly a belief in a body of truths but in a body full of love that was filled to overflowing on the first Easter day.

Ever since the first Pentecost day, God's love has been pouring out of Jesus and into all who freely choose to receive it, drawing us into the fullness of life that is fully embodied in his Risen Body. It is here alone that we are all destined 'to live and move and have our being' (Acts 17:28) and to experience something of the ecstatic bliss that Jesus experiences now and in all eternity. This is another reason why the fish symbolised Christians in the early Church.

They came to see and understand that the love of God was for them what the sea is for the fish—the living environment outside of which they could not exist. St Augustine deepens this analogy, substituting a living sponge for the fish to show that we are not only surrounded at all times by the love of God but are penetrated through and through by his all-pervading presence.

Once all the subline truths of Christ's continual and abiding presence within us are realised, there seems to be only one thing a person can do: make an act of total abandonment to God.

Express your faith in God's power and mercy:

Father, I know and believe that you are all loving and that your love has been permanently transformed into human loving through the human nature of your Son, Jesus. I know and believe that his love is perpetually poised to possess me at this moment and at every moment. Penetrate and possess me now. Permeate my whole being as I try to turn and remain open to receive you. Melt my heart of stone, remake it and remould it so that it can at all times be open to receive you. For I, unless you enthral me, never shall be free, nor ever chaste except you ravish me. Amen.

5. Abandonment to God

The trouble is that we have grown up in a world where nominal or part-time Christians abound, and honestly, we are probably numbered amongst them. The early Christians had no problem abandoning themselves to God totally, as the man to whom they committed themselves did throughout his life on earth. They knew what was being asked of them from the beginning. While they were under instruction several times a week and praying five times a day, they were witnessing the Christians, whom they were being prepared to join, giving their lives for their belief in Jesus.

Indeed, in the days of the early Church, you would not have become a Christian unless you had counted the cost, and that cost may mean losing all your property, all your wealth and your health, too, in terrible prison conditions. Here, torture was to be expected, followed by the most hideous forms of death imaginable. In short, no one became a Christian without deciding to abandon their life to God totally, no matter what the cost.

Give your all to the Almighty:

Father, you have freely chosen to share your own inner life and love with me now through Jesus as a foretaste of the ecstatic joy that you have planned for me and for all who love you in heaven. As there is no limit to the way you have poured out your loving goodness and mercy on me, I can only totally abandon myself to you in return. I, therefore, solemnly consecrate every moment of every day to you and to your honour and glory, in and together with your Son, Jesus Christ. Amen.

6. Thanksgiving

The next letter, 'T', in the memory jog, reminds us to make an Act of Thanksgiving to God for all he has given us and continues to give us. However, if we thank God only for what he has done for us or for what we have managed to get out of him, then we have not thanked him as we should. We should thank him for being God—for being goodness, justice, truth, and beauty, for displaying his own inner glory in the glory of creation surrounding us. And we should thank him for the masterpiece of creation, our Risen Lord, in and through whom we are continually being drawn up to share in his own inner life and love, beginning even in this life and then in his everlasting glory in the next.

Take your favourite prayer or hymn of thanksgiving or praise, such as the 'Gloria' from the liturgy, for instance. Recite it slowly and prayerfully, and you will find you are taken out of yourself, out of your world and into God's world where you praise him, thank him, and give him glory with all those who have learned to thank God just for being God.

Thanking God for being God leads into the heights of prayer, where thanksgiving leads to praise, and praise leads to glorifying God. Then glorifying God leads to adoration, whereby we just want to gaze upon him with a profound reverence and awe that takes us out of ourselves, if only for a time, into brief moments of bliss.

Without us realising fully what has been happening, our thanksgiving, praising, glorifying, and adoring has paved the way for a sublime spiritual highway for our love to enter into God and His love to enter into us in a way and on a level that has not happened in quite the same way before.

Give thanks to God, who gives us all things good:

Father, although you are infinitely distant, you are infinitely near, too, for you inhabit the inner marrow of my being. I thank you for being with me and for all you have given me today, for life itself and all and everyone who has made it worth living. Give me the grace to praise, honour, and thank you as much as I am able and more than I am able, not just in words but in a life that I freely dedicate to you. Amen.

7. Holy Communion

This leads us to the next letter in the blueprint, 'H', for Holy Communion. Perhaps the most holy and all-absorbing and spiritually fulfilling moment in the Mass is that sacred moment after we have received Christ internally. It is then that we silently reflect on what 'He who is mighty has done for us'.

This moment can be replicated each day in our daily prayer when we pause after giving our heartfelt thanks to God to relish what he continually gives us. This gratitude has come to be called a spiritual communion. Now is the time to ruminate on and relish the profound mysteries at work deep down within us and to digest and assimilate their sublime meaning and importance for us now and for our future.

It is time, too, to allow these truths to percolate through, to penetrate our hearts and minds, and then gaze for as long as possible at the indescribable mysteries that Jesus came to share with us.

Offer these words with Holy Communion:

Jesus, at the Last Supper, you promised to make your home in all who would obey your new commandments. Help me to obey them now and at every moment of my life. For, when I love the Father and love my neighbour as you did, there is nothing to stop you from making your home in me and me making mine in you. Let the joy and the peace that comes from abiding in you suffuse all I say and do so that others may be drawn into the Holy Communion that begins in this life and comes to its completion in the next. Amen.

Now, remain still and silent for a few moments of contemplation to relish what or, rather, whom we receive in this Holy Communion. A short prayer could be repeated gently whenever distractions threaten to draw attention elsewhere. A prayer such as 'Come Lord' or 'Come, Lord Jesus' would be ideal, or another short prayer of your choosing.

8. Examination of Conscience

At the very beginning of every Mass, we start by examining our consciences. We do this so we can see ever more clearly the sin and the selfishness which can prevent us from offering ourselves to God with a 'pure and humble heart' and can prevent us from receiving his love in return.

What happens on the day we go to celebrate Mass with the whole Catholic community should also happen every day of our lives. For, if we are going to imitate Christ and the way he lived his life, then we must endeavour to make every day of our lives into a sacrifice as Jesus himself did, offering everything that he said and did to His Father and receiving his love in return.

Whilst staying for a brief time at a Cistercian monastery, I met the holiest man I have ever known. He had been in spiritual darkness for many years. Then, one day, he became ill and was admitted to the monastery infirmary, where he received Holy Communion each day. On three distinct occasions, just as he was about to receive communion, he heard these words: 'Only you have been keeping Me out.'

We are doing exactly the same, which is why the blueprint's letter 'E' reminds us to examine our consciences each day, to pause for a few moments to review our lives since we last prayed. It is time to ask God to show us everything we have done or failed to do which has kept him out.

Let us pray to remove all obstacles which hinder us from uniting to God:

Lord, that I may see so that all that prevents me from making your home in me may be spirited away. Strengthen me to live the new commandments as you lived them so that the same Holy Spirit who filled you, guided you and raised you from the dead may do the same for me. Show me the sins that keep you out and give me the power to overcome them, for without you, I have no power to do anything. Amen.

9. Repentance

After this has been done, it is time to repent by making an Act of Contrition for how we have failed in the past. A formal act of contrition could be used, or perhaps the recitation of what came to be called the 'Jesus Prayer' said several times over, slowly and prayerfully – 'Jesus, Son of God, have mercy on me, a sinner'.

A sincere expression of personal sorrow in our own words would be better still. Then, we could make a firm purpose of amendment, a genuine decision to try and behave better in future. Finally, as we become more aware of the moral stumbling blocks that trip us up, it is time to try and forestall them. If there is a lazy streak in us or if we have a hot temper or are prone to making unkind remarks at the expense of others, resolve to take the necessary steps to avoid falling into these same faults in the forthcoming day, and pray for God's help to do what we cannot do without him.

The sort of daily prayer that Our Lady learnt from her mother and that was later perfected after her dear Son's glorification was the backbone of her prayer life, as our morning and evening prayer, inspired by and based on hers, should be for us. It will be particularly helpful when, as we shall see, clouds are gathering in our spiritual journey, and all other forms of prayer seem nearly impossible. This prayer taught to many of us by our mothers, like Mary to her Son Jesus, can be invaluable, most particularly when as St Teresa of Avila put it, 'the well runs dry'.

It is important to emphasise this assistance when new converts join the Church because they have had a conversion experience, or what is called in the Greek, Metanoia, and they all too often get ahead of themselves. They immediately take upon themselves important roles for which they consider themselves suited. However, the Greek word Metanoia means a change of mind; meanwhile, the Aramaic word used by St Peter on the first Pentecost means a continual and ongoing change of heart and of mind. Presumably with the best will in the world, they rush out to use their expertise to change their new home with their newfound fervour; nevertheless, they would be better advised to follow the example of St Paul. They should rather rush out into the desert for some years to learn and practise the prayers, the meditation, and the contemplation that will alone equip them to do what St Paul did. Here, they should be first grounded in the same sort of daily prayer that Our Lady herself practised before and after her Son's glorification. Then, when 'the well does run dry', as it certainly will, there will be a daily pattern of prayer on which to fall back to prevent them from going astray.

Turn to God the Father:

Father, I ask your forgiveness for the sins that have prevented you from possessing me as you would wish this day. I am deeply sorry for failing you yet again, and with your grace, I will never let my pride cause me to delay from turning back to you the moment I fall. Until I can love everyone as I should, help me to do them no harm and give me the sympathy and compassion of the person in whose footsteps I want to walk. Amen.

Pause briefly to review our behaviour in the past day.

Conclude with an Our Father, a Hail Mary, and a Glory Be.

When, at the end of the day, you have finished trying to pray as best you can, be at peace. You have done your best. Now, leave the rest to God, remembering the words of St Padre Pio: 'Pray, trust and don't worry.'

Chapter 26

Into the Sacred Hearts of Jesus and Mary

IN THIS CHAPTER, I want to summarise the essential teaching that I have been trying to convey in this book, because, for many, it is quite new. The dust of time and the long controversies about Mary's Immaculate Conception have sadly obfuscated what was crystal clear for the early Christians. Yet, it is essential to understand Our Lady's sublime spiritual teaching so that we learn from her if we hope to follow her example and participate as she did in the profound contemplation of her Son while preparing for the union with the Three-in-One. For, this is the ultimate destiny God has planned for us from before the dawn of time.

After many years of reflecting on his relationship with Christ and the meaning of his sublime teaching, something world-shaking happened to St John. It was a realisation that was as simple as it was infinitely profound. The emergence of this sublime epiphany was undoubtedly influenced by the Mother of God, with whom he lived for many years. What he saw in her daily life and, most particularly, in her deep contemplative prayer was decisive. She was the living, breathing embodiment of God's love, first embodied in the flesh and blood of the Son, to whom she gave birth forty or more years prior. What was embodied in her and in her Son was the love of God.

St John finally concluded, under the inspiration of the Holy Spirit, that God, therefore, must be Love. More precisely, he is loving, for he cannot but do what he is and do it all the time. So, when human beings were created in God's own image and likeness, they were made by Love to resemble himself in the very depth of their beings. However, whilst he is infinite love, or infinite loving, human beings, stigmatised by sin and selfishness, are only capable of partial, limited, or finite loving, although they crave to be united with the perfect, infinite love of God. Consequently, St Augustine said, 'Our hearts are restless until they rest in God.' How can our restless hearts come to know, love, and rest in the Love of God which we crave?

The answer is quite simple, for this is the very reason why God sent his Son, Jesus Christ, into this world on the first Christmas day. Since this epoch-making event, anyone made in the image and likeness of God can come to love God by coming to know and love him as he is embodied in the person of Jesus Christ, the Son of God. The first disciples, then, were uniquely blessed, for they could discover God's love in the most loveable, most mature, and most perfect human being who has ever lived. This, of course, was wonderful for them, but what of those who were to follow them in the first Christian and subsequent centuries? Those followers had not seen and come to love God as embodied in Jesus Christ. The answer given to the first new converts was that they should practise a new form of prayer never previously used. This new form of prayer came to be called meditation.

New converts were predominantly Jewish; therefore, they were taught, at the very minimum, to continue to pray five times a day as before. These new Christians were taught to continue to say their old prayers together with new prayers but to realise that now they were being prayed in what came to be called the Mystical Body of Christ. This gave their prayers a far greater power than before, as they were said not just in him but with him and through him to the Father.

That is why, in future, all prayers would end with different forms of 'In, with, and through Jesus Christ' because, henceforth, it would only be in, with, and through him that their love could gradually be sufficiently purified to reach out and rest in God the Father.

However, these prayers would receive their power and strength only from the measure in which they would spiritually and eventually physically be united with Jesus Christ. It would be only in this way that their human love could be united with his love, and so with him, in him, and through him, come to know and love God as he is in himself, through mystical contemplation. This contemplation became Our Lady's daily prayer immediately after the sending of the Holy Spirit on the first Pentecost day. To arrive at this profound prayer, considered the summit of the spiritual life on earth, the first Christians were taught how to meditate on the life and the loving of Jesus Christ. The more they came to know him, then the more they would come to love him, and the more their desire to be united with him would be kindled.

Although it is possible to love someone who was once alive and active in this world, it is not possible to be presently united with them. When, therefore, the desire for union with Christ has been sufficiently demonstrated in meditation, the Holy Spirit redirects our love and desire for union with him as he is now, in his Risen Glory. Then, we are led into what has been traditionally called the Mystic Way. Here, by persevering in what came to be called mystical contemplation, we are prepared for the union for which we yearn. Not exclusively, but above all else, beginners were taught how to meditate on the Passion and death of Christ because that happens to be the most perfect expression of human and divine loving that the world has ever known. In this way, their love would be enkindled, generating the love that would induce the Holy Spirit to lead them into the beginning of contemplation. Here, they would be purified for the union possible for only those who have been sufficiently purified.

The first time we see this new method of prayer called meditation mentioned was when the faithful, in addition to their other daily prayers, were told to meditate on Christ's Passion and death. They were told to practise this prayer in addition to their other prayers—at nine o'clock in the morning to coincide with Our Lord's condemnation to death, at midday when he was actually crucified, and at three o'clock when he finally died on the Cross. The faithful were reminded to do this when, according to the custom at the time, a drum would be beaten, a horn blown, a trumpet sounded, or a human voice would cry out to announce the passing of the hours.

This may not be the best or most opportune occasion for the sort of meditation which became a vital part of an early Christian's life. Nevertheless, if we wish to develop our spiritual life so that we come to know and experience the love of God, the practice of meditation must gradually become part of our lives at whatever time we can find. This is the most important form of prayer that will lead us onward and into the love of God. Meditation is where human love is gradually animated by divine love, which leads it onward and into the profound contemplation that Our Lady experienced immediately on the first Pentecost day and on subsequent days. This was to show her new children in the infant Church where their daily meditation would eventually lead them when, through practising daily repentance, they would be purified to join her. As all the great saints in subsequent centuries show by both word and example, true Christian meditation leads onwards and into contemplation.

Since his Ascension, Jesus Christ has been loving his Father ever more perfectly. This is because he is no longer hindered by the evil behaviours of those whom he came to serve to save—save from the lovelessness to which selfishness and sin condemns them.

When meditation has filled a person with the best love that we human beings can generate for God, the Holy Spirit always leads those who have persevered into the contemplative prayer that will eventually lead us into the contemplative prayer of Christ, even in this life. But, before experiencing what some have called the contemplation of light, the searcher must necessarily experience the contemplation of darkness. Although we are experiencing the contemplation of God's loving light, the all-pervading and penetrating light of his love highlights every nook and cranny where sinfulness lurks within us, preventing the loving union for which God has created us. This is the critical moment in a person's spiritual life when, as St John of the Cross lamented, ninety percent of those who have come this far turn away.

In doing this, we are turning away from the only form of prayer that can prepare us to receive what the Greek Fathers called the Pleroma, the fullness of God's love. More precisely, his Holy Spirit, who gradually draws us up and ever more deeply into the Mystical Body of Jesus, Our Risen Lord. St. John perceives this tragic error due to ignorance, mostly inculpable because, in his day but perhaps even more in our day, people are sheep without shepherds. The more we journey on with daily perseverance—come hell or high water—the more we are fitted ever more completely not just into the Mystical Body of Christ but into his mystical loving of his Father.

Here, we join our Mother Mary, who joined him in this profound mystical loving the very moment she received the Holy Spirit on the first Pentecost day. It was then that her Immaculate and Sacred Heart was joined to his Sacred Heart so that together they could be at one in giving glory to the Father. This is the new Temple into which we are all called to worship God when the new worship in Spirit and in truth is brought to perfection. As the centuries have rolled by, more and more of the faithful have been drawn into the mystical Temple, which is Christ's Mystical Body, and it is into this company that we are invited as we learn to become perfect lovers in the School of Divine Love.

Chapter 27

From Here to Epecstasy

WHEN PREPARING TO SET OFF on a journey, it is essential that you know where you are going and why. The journey I am referring to is the most important journey of all. It is the journey to our ultimate destiny: love without measure. To understand this journey, we must listen to the greatest theologian of all. Most lesser theologians consider projecting human emotions onto God neither appropriate nor helpful. However, Jesus Christ, the greatest theologian of all, begs to differ. Throughout his Gospels, he not only makes it clear that God is Love but that he wants God to be to us like an ever-loving Divine Dad. A Dad who has so loved us from the very beginning that he wants us to share in the ongoing and everlasting experience of ecstatic bliss rewarded to those who have faithfully tried to love him.

Although St Augustine said that our destiny would lead us to experience a supernatural ecstasy, the mystic poet St Gregory of Nyssa went one step further. He said that when we are drawn into divine contemplation and then into the glory of God's infinite loving, we would simply journey onward with unceasing, ever-increasing rapturous loving. For, as we are drawn relentlessly onward into the glory that expresses God's inner infinite loving, our own hearts would continually expand to facilitate the heavenly indwelling of the three divine persons within us. We would never stop growing in love, never stop receiving love, and never tire of experiencing an endless inflow of divine loving. Consequently, St Gregory of Nyssa said that we will ultimately experience not just ecstasy but epecstasy. By adding the Greek pre-fix, ep, he created a new word meaning not just ecstasy but ongoing, never-ending ecstasy. This becomes possible because, as our hearts expand to receive God's infinite loving in ever greater depth and magnitude, we never cease extending beyond ourselves to experience, in ever fuller measure, the love without measure that is God's inner life.

Just as any genuinely good person desires to share their joys with those they love, Christ told us that God 'felt' likwese. Therefore, he created us, from the very beginning, with the means that could take us from the earthly world he created for us into the heavenly world intended for our final destiny. In what he called 'the fullness of time', his only begotten Son, in whom the world was created, would himself be made flesh as its King to take us back to all that God had prepared for us to enjoy from the beginning. The Great Franciscan Theologian John Duns Scotus, born in Scotland at the end of the thirteenth century, said that when

God conceives an end, he also conceives the means to bring it about. Therefore, if God wanted his only begotten Son to be born in space and time as a perfect human being, then he must have a perfect or immaculate mother—conceived from the beginning in the mind of God—to become the Mother of God.

Yet, where does Original Sin fit into God's plan? The simple answer is that Original Sin does not fit into God's plan, nor do the sinners who are contaminated by this primaeval sin. God did not conceive Original Sin; we did. That is why Christ had to do something not initially conceived before he could lead us all back to the heaven, for which we were created. He had to save the fallen—that means all of us from the sin that has stigmatised and contaminated us with evil. He had to be our King who would lead us into his Father's Kingdom. He had to be our Saviour, too—saving us from our sinfulness and enabling us to be purified so as to be united with our perfect, infinite, loving Father.

When I travel to London, I must take what is called the London train because it has come from London and is on its way back from where it has come. This is what Christ has come to do for us. He has come from heaven, and he is going back to heaven to take with him all who have been prepared and purified for eternal living and loving. When Christ was reunited with his Father's infinite love after his Ascension, he did something for which we can only eternally thank him. He poured his love onto and into all of us on the first Pentecost day and on every subsequent day to the end of time. This love draws all who are open to receive it into his Mystical Body, brought into being after his Ascension into heaven. Now, this Mystical Body into which we are admitted at baptism becomes the mystical means by which we are transported to heaven to enjoy, with ever greater depth and intensity, God's infinite loving.

Unlike a man-made train, this mystical means of transportation is propelled by the supernatural fuel of divine love. We advance to meet our ultimate destiny with the help of the Holy Spirit as our human loving mixes, mingles, and finally merges with Christ's own divine loving. In this way, a new hybrid, hypostatic form of love is generated that can alone take us to our destiny. The more we are purified as the journey advances towards God, then the sure-er, the safer, and the quicker we travel towards epecstasy.

CHAPTER 28

THE LAST MINUTE OF EXTRA TIME

FOR OVER FOUR HUNDRED YEARS, for
reasons explained in detail elsewhere, the
profound and sublime mystical theology
teaching us how to generate the love that
can alone unite us to Christ through dying
to self has been all but absent from Catholic
mainstream spirituality. It reached its height
in the early Church and then spiked upward
again in the spirituality prevalent for over a
century following the Council of Trent. This
mystical spirituality suffused and surcharged
the Tridentine, or what we now simply call
the Latin Mass, which enabled participants
to unite their daily infused sacrificial loving
with the sacrifice of the Mass.

Then, almost out of the blue, this
ancient God-given spirituality vanished.

It vanished, never to return as our mainstream spirituality following the 1687 condemnation of Quietism. Since then, the love that every family needs for survival and prosperity has been removed from the Catholic family, or the Church, to which we belong. Consequently, without this sublime supernatural loving, our beloved Church has been languishing almost to death as all with eyes to see can see. Yes, prayerful petitions have been presented, devotions have been practised (some more efficacious than others), and praise and adoration have been offered in and out of the liturgy. But that is not enough.

Without the continual and daily reception of divine mystical loving, we have always tended to go no deeper than the superficial. That is why, sadly, the profound contemplative spirituality that we first see being brought to perfection in our Blessed Mother on the first Pentecost day and on subsequent days has all but vanished. Unfortunately, this sublime God-given spirituality that brought about the union of her Sacred Heart with the Sacred Heart of Jesus has been set aside in favour of a plethora of miscellaneous devotional practices from which the faithful have been choosing their own individual and personalised spiritualities. It is time to return to the God-given spirituality that Our Lord himself introduced into the early Church—the spirituality lived and handed on by Our Blessed Mother to the infant Church.

This is what the great reforming councils, such as the Fourth Lateran Council and the Council of Trent, did in the past. These councils were successful because they were all preceded and inspired by so many great saints and mystics (plus new religious orders and congregations) who remain household names to this day. The Second Vatican Council, however, was tragically devoid of such saints and new vibrant religious orders. Indeed, old and once-respected religious orders have depleted on a scale never before witnessed. Additionally, so many of those who have remained behind have been convicted of unthinkable, heinous crimes or have lived clandestine lives where chastity is daily flouted. When love moves out, evil moves in. If it is by their fruits that you will know them, then neither Christ nor his Church wants to know them except in sackcloth and ashes. As we can now all observe, an unfortunate and albeit unforeseen legacy of the Second Vatican Council is that it is leading to a Church that, as Our Lady has predicted, is about to implode. That is because heretical doctrines are being openly accepted to replace the ancient and sacred Church traditions designed by God. Such Tradition was designed to reflect on earth his Kingdom in heaven.

Inspired by the words of Pope St John Paul II's great 1995 exhortation, Ut unum Sint – 'That they may be one' – let us all unite together by returning to the spirituality first lived and then introduced into the early Church.

If we do not unite, then the faithful will be split into splinter groups like the first protestants, always at war with one another. This is the spirituality lived to perfection, practised, and handed on to others by Our Lady, the Mother of God herself, before being assumed into heaven. This is the spirituality I have been studying, trying to practise, and striving to hand on to others in all that I have lectured and written about over the last sixty-five years. It is not my spirituality; it is God's spirituality. All I have attempted is to restate it: how it was first given to us in the early Church and then later supplemented by great saints and mystics through whom the Holy Spirit still speaks to us. This is our ancient and hallowed tradition to which we must promptly return with pure and humble hearts. The existential philosopher

Kierkegaard said that purity of heart is to will one thing. Let this one thing be to return together to the God-given spirituality that Jesus Christ bequeathed to the early Church and that his beloved mother perfectly embodied here on earth.

We may well be residing in the last minute of extra time. However, that does not mean we lack time to change our lives and begin again. Remember the good thief on the cross. Whilst recalling this, we must cleave to one another whilst at the same time staying together as God's remnant to stand together against the monstrous evil forces occupying the Church's highest offices who are arraigned against us. Remember, the gates of Hell will not ultimately prevail against Christ's Bride, the Church, but they will and are currently prevailing against numerous one-time shepherds. Evil and devilish powers are even now bent on 'reforming'—or, to put it more accurately, reimagining—the

Church, not into God's image and likeness but into their own depraved, self-centred, pleasure-seeking, anti-philosophy of narcissism for all. If Our Lady is to be believed—and I, for one, do believe her—then even they will be given one last chance. And so will we.

Now is the time to prepare for that last chance so that when it is given, we have already begun to do for ourselves what we must then do for the depraved and deluded world. We must return to the destiny for which God made the world in the beginning—that the prayer of ages will, at last, be seen embodied in us. Then, finally, God's Kingdom will be seen embodied here on earth as it is in heaven. Here, Christ will ultimately rule as King and his mother will rule as Queen. And their Sacred Hearts, made one, will draw all to join them in the heavenly liturgy, giving praise, adoration, and glory to God. He is the infinitely loving and magnanimous God, our Divine Dad, who has called us to experience with him the rapturous bliss of never-ending ecstatic union, or what St Gregory of Nyssa called Epecstasy, to the end of time, together with all whom we love and hold dear.

CHAPTER 29

THE CORONATION AND ITS CONSEQUENCES

WE TEND TO BELIEVE that when Our Lady's Assumption and Coronation as Queen of Heaven marked the final glorious consummation of the life of the most illustrious woman who has ever lived. This honour was God's supreme gift to the woman he conceived as the mother of his only begotten Son.

The truth, however, is far more profound and sublime. A coronation celebrates not an end but a new beginning. A monarch is invested with God-given power, ushering in ongoing spiritual and physical development for the person themselves and for those in their regal care. God's power, and the power bestowed upon any Christian monarch, is love. The fons et origo—the source and fountainhead—of this love may be found as an infinite vortex of supernatural life and loving. This vivacious exchange binds the three persons of the Holy Trinity—the source and destiny of all other life, both spiritual and material. When Our Lady was crowned in heaven, it was not just God's reward for a life perfectly lived in his Name, but the mark of a new departure in her vocation—her calling as his specially chosen Mother for his Son and for his Church. It was to draw her ever more closely to himself, to receive in ever greater measure the love without measure that he wanted to continually bestow on her for herself and, through her, onto countless others on earth for whom she was destined to be a Mother to the end of time. Regardless of all the praises given, all the blessings bestowed, and all the honours awarded to our Blessed Mother, she remains mortal like ourselves in all things except sin. She is still finite in her origin and in her person. Thus, her journey, like our journey into the infinite and inexhaustible love of the Three-in-One, is eternally ongoing, evermore captivating, and eternally enthralling. As more and more of her children join her, in, with and through her beloved Son in his glorified and transformed humanity, they join her on her unending journey to epecstasy. What a homecoming has Christ prepared for us, in him and with his Immaculate Mother and with St Joseph! With her human family now united again like never before, all other human families are invited to join them, as countless millions of faithful followers in her wake. With her and in her Son, they journey onward towards the family of the three infinite and everlasting lovers bound together as one Family. They are the source and destiny of all other families, thanks to the perfect God-given Son who laid down his human life so that supernatural life may be available to all.

Lest there is any misunderstanding, be sure that we are not travelling to our destiny with Mary and Joseph in their beloved Son as some sort of disembodied spirits. We are not Gnostics but Christians who, like Christ on Mount Tabor, will experience the total regeneration of our whole personalities—body and blood, soul and humanity. Nor, therefore, will our individual personalities evaporate into some sort of disembodied pantheistic paradise where we lose our identity as we dissipate into the Absolute. The greater the love, the more we gravitate toward our true selves and thus veer from the self-centred selves who began the journey. Therefore, our whole human being (not just our souls) shall be continually perfected in the infinite love without measure, which unceasingly permeates and penetrates every part of our personalities. Our own personal joy is multiplied by seeing those whom we have loved on earth become their true selves. Encountering them in their glory, we love them even more than they ever thought possible. This is because everyone endlessly advances into the epecstatic bliss of the beatific union, where all families find their consummation. This Family expresses itself in the infinite love that bonds the three divine persons as one is the uncreated Family that is the origin and destiny of all other families.

Far from enjoying her own eternal destiny as it unfolds with ever more and all-engrossing delights, our heavenly Mother's thoughts are simultaneously with her children on earth. She burns with what is now a supernatural love to ensure that as many as possible join her in the utterly captivating thrill and joy of being possessed by love without measure. Our Lady was possessed by the fruits of contemplation whilst on earth; therefore, these supernatural, infused virtues and gifts must necessarily grow even more, as the one who first generated them in her possesses her with ever-increasing loving.

She seemingly forgoes the ecstatic delight of supernatural contemplation temporarily to forewarn her children on earth of the hellbent destination to which their self-bent actions are leading them.

Mary has revealed herself predominantly to children, presumably because the vast majority of contemporary adults are all too preoccupied with self to consider or comprehend our Immaculate Mother's pure, simple, and uncomplicated words. Even modern believers have managed to completely isolate themselves from God's Word because they have minimized to the nominal what is a rather superficial prayer life. Our Lady promised the children at Fatima that in the 'final times' of this era that is approaching, her gift to the Church would be her Immaculate Heart, overflowing with love for all who are open to receive it. It would seem, then, that in these end times that are now upon us, the love that her

Sacred Heart received from her Son's Sacred Heart can save us. In these terrible times, God has determined that it shall be one of us—Mary Immaculate, whom he exalted as our heavenly Queen—who will be the mediatrix of the only love capable of saving the world from damnation.

Chapter 30

The Final Battle

THE POWER OF LOVE and the power of evil are already locked in a battle. The prize will be a new world order in which there can be only two possible outcomes: either good will triumph over evil, or evil will triumph over good. This battle is already raging in the Church. The Goths are no longer at the gates, but they are in the precincts of Rome itself, preparing to turn right and wrong on its head.

Winston Churchill once said that until the world is ruled by love, it must be chained by law. Anyone who listens to the religious or the secular news today cannot fail to recognize that what we perceived in our youth as inviolable laws and moral imperatives are being subtly but systematically dismantled. Divine laws, Christ's laws, natural, moral, religious, secular, and civil laws are being dismantled in the name of a cunning interior revolution, stealthily introduced to create a new world order completely opposed to that which Christ came to inaugurate. For this new order, the first and supreme law is utter, unbridled, unrestricted 'liberty' – better termed anarchy—so that everyone is unhindered from indulging in whatever depravity they desire. Furthermore, they seek allowances to preach this new gospel in every educational institution, from infant schools to the schools of elite learning. Naysayers must be cancelled and severely punished. In this new world order, only egality and fraternity exist for those who have rejected all laws, all standards, and all morals and manners which once made human society possible. The rest are consigned to oblivion or modern versions of the guillotine. Disaster awaits us. It is inevitably upon us unless we receive, welcome, and assimilate in these final moments of 'injury time' the love endlessly flowing from the Queen of Heaven's Sacred Heart. Do we proclaim ourselves as believers? Are we believers who want with all our hearts and minds, bodies and souls and all their strength to receive our Blessed Mother's God-given love as manna from heaven? If we continue to reject this divine love she brings, then the already budding anarchy will overwhelm both the Catholic Church and the world she was once committed to transforming.

I want to end by following Our Lady's lead, repeating and explaining one last time the simple message that she has been giving us. This message alone can save us from the perdition into which we witness our one-time shepherds, mentors, and leaders falling. A person may be converted by intellectual or emotional conviction or a bit of both, either through God's direct intervention or by some supernatural action. These are far from uncommon experiences, although not usually so dramatic as that of St Paul. People may be converted after a long lapse from their inherited faith, but they will all then be called upon to hear and put into practice the words St Peter spoke on the first Pentecost day. It is the same call that Our Lady herself used whenever she appeared in recent times. It is the call to repentance, followed by the call to prayer, sacrifice, and participation in the sacrifice of the Mass.

The Irish 'present continuing tense', unknown in the English language, best shows how we should repent. If put into English, it is best translated as – 'I have repented, I am repenting, and I will continue to repent.' This, in fact, embodies the meaning of the Aramaic or the Hebrew word for repentance better than any other. Once we have committed ourselves to repentance—to continually turning back to God for the rest of our lives—then we must commit to an ongoing, ever-continuing process. However, if this act is to be successful, this repentance must be fortified, strengthened, and surcharged by the continual inflowing of God's love. And God's love must be received, developed, and perfected in daily prayer. Here, our weak human love is continually raised to God, and his loving descends into our loving. Then, gradually, through perseverance and purification, our personal loving is penetrated, permeated, and then perfected by divine loving. This transformation occurs as our love mixes, mingles, and ultimately merges with the Holy Spirit and overflows into our total and complete human personality.

To facilitate this holy and sacred action, we must reconstruct our lives. Such reconstruction must allow us to daily enjoy sufficient quality space and time for what St Angela of Foligno called the School of

Divine Love. Here, human and divine loving mutually compenetrate each other to the glory of God in heaven and to the glory and extension of his Church on earth. The sacrifices involved in facilitating this mystical union will be the most important sacrifices we bring to Mass each Sunday when our newly formed love enables us to be united with the love that Christ continually offers to his Father. I am speaking of the sacrifices we have made while attempting to deny ourselves everything that prevents us from placing our love of God above all every day of our lives as we practice repentance in prayer.

In order to keep God's commandments, we must keep turning to prayer. In prayer—in concentrated periods of time set aside for that purpose that we keep trying to raise our hearts and minds to God—four things always follow. For, 'In the trying is the dying, and in the dying is the purifying, and in the purifying is the unifying' with the God who gives his love to us as we try to give our love to him. The sacrifices that we make unite us with Christ's great sacrifice in the Mass, where his life of self-sacrifice that we celebrate at Mass becomes the place where all we say and do is offered through him to the Father.

This is what Our Lady herself did every day of her life after the Holy Spirit had taken her up into Christ's Mystical Body on that first Pentecost day. She became the perfect example to all the early Christians of what they should do to enter with her into her beloved Son and into his relentless loving of his Father. Here, with her, we will gradually enter more deeply into Christ's sublime contemplation of the Father. It is here, whilst still on earth, that we will receive the fruits of that divine contemplation, without which the pagan world would never have been transformed into Christianity. She has returned in modern times on God's behalf to spread the same message which God first proclaimed when Christianity was in its first flush of fervour. Today, however, her call to repentance is not to herald the first beginnings of Christ's Church but its abrupt and ignominious destruction from within should her message remain unheeded.

I said at the beginning of this book that her simple message was far too difficult for theologians to understand and so put into practice. That is why it has taken me a whole book to explain them to myself. I can only hope that others who began like me will be given the humility to listen to little children. Let us now put into practice the simple but eminently profound and sublime message that has been given to and understood by little children, unfettered by the pretentious sophistication that blinds even the most meticulously manicured minds to the mind of God.

May we pray in the words of Matthew's chapter 11, verse 25: 'I praise You, Father, Lord of heaven and earth that You have hidden these things, these spiritual truths from the wise and intelligent and revealed them to little children'.

Hail Mary, full of grace,
the Lord is with thee.
Blessed art thou among women,
and blessed is the fruit of thy womb, Jesus.

Holy Mary, Mother of God,
pray for us sinners,
now and at the hour of our death.
Amen.

Our Lady of Mount Carmel, pray for us.

Mary conceived without sin, pray for us.

About This Book

To the humiliation of modern man, many more people have journeyed on pilgrimage to Marian Shrines over the past century than the number who dedicated their lives to Christianity in the first century after the Resurrection. The lamentation here is not that contemporary people made the journey but rather that the pilgrimage did not affect their hearts thoroughly. If only they had done for the modern world what the first Christians did for the ancient pagan world, then Our Lady would not have had to keep returning to warn us that God is poised to punish our world for failing to listen to her. The difference is that we think we can have it both ways. We think that we can continue to enjoy the material pleasures of the pagan world in which we live while continuing to enjoy the spiritual benefits of our Catholic faith. Our first Christian forebears knew they could not. Using the mystery of her Immaculate Conception as his guide, the author leads us back to understand, love and, ultimately embrace the God-given spirituality that Jesus Christ introduced into the early Church.

About the Author

David Torkington has spent over sixty years of his life studying and trying to live the profoundly mystical teaching of early Christianity. Thanks to circumstances that were not of his making, he came to see and understand that when a Christian is taken up into the Mystical Body of Christ, this is but the beginning. It is the prelude to years of purification that can alone unite us with Christ's sublime loving of his Father through what St Thomas Aquinas called mystical contemplation. This book details how the first great Christian mystic—Mary the Immaculate Mother of God, who was the first to experience and receive the fruits of mystical contemplation on the first Pentecost day—inspired and guided all who would follow her. As one who is currently living in what he calls the winter of his discontent, he believes rediscovering mystical contemplation

315

is the only hope for thwarting the spiritual anarchy presently usurping the contemporary Church. It is the sole remedy that can precipitate what St John Henry Newman promised would be 'A new Spring' after the prolonged dark night which has for all too long enveloped us.

https://www.davidtorkington.com

www.ingramcontent.com/pod-product-compliance
Lightning Source LLC
Chambersburg PA
CBHW030912090426
42737CB00007B/168